C000253999

Chronology 8

Britannia 9
Carausius • *Barbarica conspiratio* • Stilicho • Constantinus

Design 18
Construction methods • Raw materials • Human resources

Anatomy 24
Defences • Brancaster-*Branoduno* • Caister-on-Sea • Burgh Castle-*Gariannum*
Walton Castle • Bradwell-*Othona* • Reculver-*Regulbium* • Richborough-*Rutupiae*
Dover-*Dubris* • Lympne-*Lemanis* • Pevensey-*Anderitum* • Portchester-*Portus Adurni*

Function 38
Notitia Dignitatum • Anti-pirate defence • Defence against Rome • Fortified ports

Occupation 46
Internal buildings • Garrisons • Extra-mural activity • Twilight years

The sites today 58
Brancaster • Caister-on-Sea • Burgh Castle • Walton Castle • Bradwell
Reculver • Richborough • Dover • Lympne • Pevensey
Porchester • Useful contact information

Glossary 62

Bibliography 63

Index 64

Introduction

At Richborough-*Rutupiae* stood the 'Great Monument', the symbolic gateway to the new province of Britannia. This was a magnificent four-way arch, towering 25m high and lavishly adorned with bronze statuary and marble specially imported from Italy. Richborough-*Rutupiae* was the chief port of Britannia, at least during the 1st century AD, and the monument was evidently a piece of imperial propaganda designed to impress the many visitors passing through. It was placed here because it was at or near Richborough-*Rutupiae* that the invading forces had first landed.

By the mid-3rd century AD this grandiose icon of Roman imperial power had been stripped of all its adornments and converted into a watchtower protected by an earthen rampart and triple ditches. By then a new foe had appeared in the form of pirates, the fore runners of the Saxon settlers of later times, who were coming in across the foggy waters of the northern seas. Shortly afterwards the monument was totally levelled, the earth bank slighted, and the ditches were filled in when the walls of the Saxon Shore fort were built.

The name 'Saxon Shore' itself is ambiguous: it could be interpreted as the 'shore settled by Saxons' (White 1961) rather than as the 'shore attacked by Saxons' (Johnson 1979). When the Romano-Vandal generalissimo Flavius Stilicho was active in Britannia, the name was used to describe, in a document known as the *Notitia Dignitatum*, a system of bases on what was clearly called a *limes* – frontier. This document is a late Roman collection of administrative information, which includes lists of civil and military officials and of military units and their forts. Thus under the command of an officer described as *comes litoris Saxonici per Britanniam* – count of the Saxon Shore in Britannia – fell nine units in nine named forts (*ND Occ.* XXVIII$_{13-21}$).

It is assumed, therefore, that the bases had a defensive military function associated with harbours and a fleet with which they were designed to liaise. A Roman fleet (*classis Britannica*) had been based in Britannia from the 2nd century AD at the latest. Vegetius, writing at the end of the 4th century AD, indicates that such a fleet still existed when he describes (*Epit.* 4.37) the camouflaged, scouting-skiffs of the Romano-British navy on patrol against invasion or infiltration. Thus the military installations of the Saxon Shore are closely bound up with the history of the fleet, though this does not mean the system arose fully fledged as part of a single master plan, which is the unfortunate and false impression given by the *Notitia Dignitatum*.

Although the exact dates of construction of the so-called Saxon Shore forts are uncertain, the development of the Wash–Solent *limes* was spread over at least a century and thus was not planned all at the same time as a concerted series of fortifications. Many of the new forts were notable for the increased size of their defences, with thicker masonry walls studded with forward-projecting towers to take artillery, and other features clearly designed to make them more difficult to storm than old-style frontier forts with their classic playing-card shape and internal angle- and interval-turrets. Defence, in the Principate, had meant aggressive response or even offensive pre-emptive strike into enemy territory before there could be any attack on Roman installations. The new trend was to build stronger, the emphasis being on grimly determined defence as opposed to precautionary protection. Most of the major harbours and estuaries of the south and east coasts of Britannia were now fortified in this manner. There was also a similar series of military installations in Gaul, extending along the northern coast as far as Armorica, or what is now Brittany.

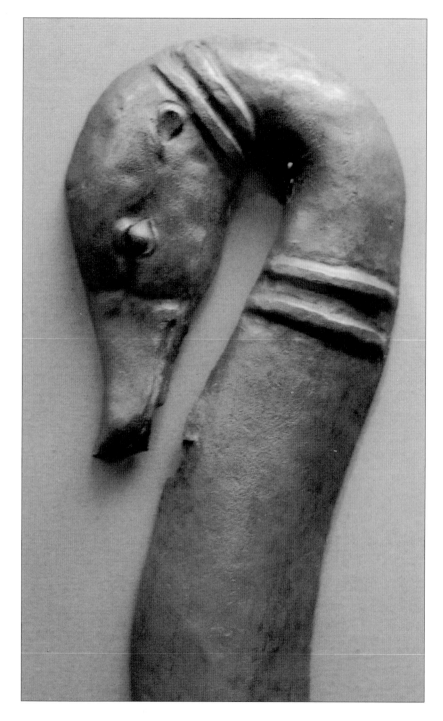

Bronze goose-head (London, British Museum, PRB1950.4-2.1) from Richborough, which once decorated the stem-post of a Roman warship. The bird was sacred to the Egyptian moon-goddess, Isis, patron deity of seafarers. (Esther Carré)

Whatever their true tactical and strategic function, a debate that is still in progress amongst scholars, the construction of these forts represents a huge outlay of money, manpower and materials. The Saxon Shore forts (the term will be used throughout for sake of convenience), among the most impressive surviving monuments of Roman Britain, remain therefore an open question. Recent scholarship, rather than viewing them as garrison forts in the conventional manner, has placed much greater emphasis on what is termed the socio-economic aspects of the monuments, consequently downgrading the Saxons, as sea-raiders, to a nagging, intermittent threat.

Provincial capital
Military installation

0   50 miles

0   100km

N

Wash–Solent *limes*
The system of forts that
made up the landward
defences of the Saxon
Shore was designed to
deter seaborne raids from
across the 'northern seas'.

OCEANUS
GERMANICUS

CALEDONIA

Antonine Wall

Hadrian's Wall

Eboracum ■

Lancaster ●

BRITANNIA
SECUNDA

HIBERNIA

FLAVIA
CAESARIENSIS

Lindum ■

Branoduno ●

Caister-on-Sea ●
Gariannum

MAXIMA
CAESARIENSIS

Walton Castle ●

Othona ●

Cardiff ●   Corinium ■
     Dobunnorum

Londinium ■

Regulbium ●
Rutupiae ●
Dubris ●

BRITANNIA
PRIMA

Portus Adurni ●   Lemanis ●

Anderitum ●

Gesoriacum ●
Bononia

OCEANUS BRITANNICUS

GALLIA

Nowadays it seems fashionable to view the Saxon Shore forts as little more than fortified ports, essential links in a provincial logistical system concerned with troop movements and the exploitation of natural and agricultural resources in Britannia. And so significant doubt is cast on the documentary evidence for maritime attacks on the south and east coasts of Britannia. Still, just because the Graeco-Roman sources are silent or ambiguous we cannot simply assume that piracy was not taking place. Writings that discuss Britannia are scant, and the problem of a maritime threat to the island could easily have been passed over by contemporary authors writing from Rome or elsewhere in the empire. It is indeed curious if such powerful defences were intended to be no more than in transient and occasional use. The reality of the raids, or at least, the perception of a threat, need not be doubted.

The Roman curtains and towers of Portchester-*Portus Adurni* were later incorporated into the defences of a Norman keep. The fabric of the walls is entirely of Roman work though refaced in places, as shown here in this view of the fort's east circuit. (Esther Carré)

Chronology

AD 284	Accession of Diocletianus	AD 379	Theodosius I proclaimed emperor
AD 286	Maximian appointed co-emperor	AD 382	Magnus Maximus checks incursion of Picti and Scotti
AD 287	Carausius seizes Britannia		
AD 293	Tetrarchy formed – Constantius Chlorus and Galerius proclaimed Caesars	AD 383	Magnus Maximus proclaimed in Britannia – eliminates Gratianus in Gaul
	Carausius' forces expelled from Boulogne-sur-Mer (*Gesoriacum Bononia*)	AD 384	Flavius Stilicho marries niece of Theodosius – promoted to *comes domesticorum*
	Carausius assassinated by Allectus	AD 388	Defeat and execution of Magnus Maximus – Valentinianus II 'western emperor'
AD 296	Britannia recovered by Constantius Chlorus – major repairs to Hadrian's Wall	AD 391	Theodosius bans all pagan worship
	Britannia becomes a diocese of four provinces	AD 392	Death of Valentinianus – Arbogastes raises Eugenius as usurper in west
AD 297	Picti first mentioned by name as raiding northern Britannia	AD 394	Battle of Frigidus (Wippach) in Pannonia – Theodosius regains control of empire
AD 305	Diocletianus abdicates – causes Maximian to do the same		Stilicho western generalissimo (*magister peditum praesentalis*)
AD 306	Constantius I Chlorus campaigns in Caledonia	AD 395	Death of Theodosius – empire split between east (Arcadius) and west (Honorius)
	Constantius dies at York-*Eboracum* – Constantinus I proclaimed emperor	AD 398	Victories over Picti, Scotti and Saxones – troop withdrawals from Britannia
AD 312	Constantinus' victory over Maximian's son Maxentius at Milvian Bridge	AD 406	Marcus proclaimed in Britannia
			Vandals, Suevi and Alans cross Rhine into Gaul
AD 313	Christianity tolerated by Edict of Milan	AD 407	Constantinus III proclaimed in Britannia – crosses into Gaul
AD 324	Constantinus sole emperor – foundation of Constantinople (Istanbul)	AD 408	Stilicho falls to a palace coup and executed
AD 333	Constantinus appoints as Caesar his son Constans	AD 409	Britannia revolts from Constantinus – end of Roman rule in Britannia
AD 337	Death of Constantinus		Vandals, Suevi and Alans enter Iberia
AD 343	Constans visits Britannia	AD 410	Alaric takes Rome – allows his men to pillage the city for three days
AD 350	Constans ousted by army		
	Proclamation of Magnentius in Gaul – seizes Britannia		Honorius tells Romano-Britons to look to their own defences
AD 353	Defeat and suicide of Magnentius – Constantius II recovers Gaul and Britannia	AD 411	Constantinus defeated at Arles (*Arelate*)
		AD 425	Flavius Aëtius in Gaul as *magister militum per Gallias*
AD 355	Iulianus (the Apostate) appointed Caesar – governs Gaul and Britannia	AD 429	Germanus, bishop of Autessiodurum (Auxerre), visits Britannia
AD 360	Iulianus II sole emperor – official revival of paganism	AD 446	Appeal of Romano-Britons to Aëtius (Gildas)
	Incursion of Picti and Scotti – expedition of *magister militum* Flavius Lupicinus	AD 449	Arrival of 'the English' in Britain (Bede)
AD 364	Valentinianus I proclaimed emperor	AD 451	Hun invasion of Gaul checked by Aëtius at Châlons
AD 367	*Barbarica conspiratio*		
AD 368	Flavius Theodosius sent to recover Britannia – Hadrian's Wall restored	AD 454	Murder of Aëtius – western army subsequently run down
AD 375	Death of Valentinianus	AD 469	Romano-British army under Riothamus defends Aquitania Prima
AD 378	Destruction of eastern army at Hadrianopolis (Edirne) – Valens killed	AD 476	Romulus Augustus deposed by Odoacer

Britannia

The assassination of Severus Alexander (AD 235) ushered in an unparalleled era of political and economic chaos. The ending of the Severan dynasty left no clear successor, and there was not an established mechanism by which a new emperor was to be selected. This institutional weakness was to be mercilessly exposed over the following five decades, during which time over 60 individuals, many of them adventurers, would lay claim to the imperial title. This was the time when a provincial soldier could rise to the top and enjoy a brief and violent reign. Thus one usurper followed the next, and only one emperor, Claudius II (r. AD 268–70), actually died of natural causes. However, despite the cycle of regicide and military insurrections, Britannia appears to have been comparatively tranquil.

Instigated by the Illyrian soldier-emperor Diocletianus (r. AD 284–305), the tendency to separate military and civilian careers was complete under Constantinus I (r. AD 306–37). The provincial governors (*praesides*), now stripped of military authority, had greater administrative responsibilities. Henceforth each province had both a civil governor (*praes*) and a military commander (*dux*). This separation of military authority would thus make it more difficult for military commanders to revolt, since they would need to secure the support of the now separate civil authority. Likewise, the removal of civilian responsibilities would ease the promotion of competent men within the army, since the lack of a literary education would no longer now matter. The way was now open for the rise of men such as Flavius Stilicho.

The Roman world would never be the same place after Diocletianus and his reforms. This stylized porphyry group (Rome, Vatican Library) portrays two members (Diocletianus and Galerius, or Maximian and Constantius) of the Tetrarchy not as persons but as identical types in a soldierly embrace. (Author's collection)

To further limit the possibility of military insurrection, Diocletianus also reorganized the running of the empire. His solution was to create 12 dioceses, or administrative units, each governed by a *vicarius* representing one of the two praetorian prefects, who now lost their military role and became heads of the civil administration. These acted as deputies to the two Caesars, who in turn were subordinate to the two Augusti. Each diocese was divided into provinces, which had been reduced in size and greatly enlarged in number.

According to a document of AD 314 (*Lacterculus Veronensis* vii, cf. *ND Occ.* XXIII$_{9-15}$) the Diocese of Britanniae comprised four provinces, with the diocesan capital at London-*Londinium*. In the east lay the provinces of Maxima Caesariensis and Flavia Caesariensis. To the west of these provinces lay Britannia Prima and, to the north of all these, Britannia Secunda. Another province, Valentia, is known but may have been one of the former provinces re-named. The provincial capitals were large Roman towns. Within these provinces were smaller political divisions, *civitates*, each with its own capital. Again these were major Roman towns, provided with fortification walls, public buildings and at least one forum. Whether Christian or pagan, by the 4th century AD the whole free population of the diocese were considered citizens (*cives*) of the empire at birth, and any division between 'Romans' and 'Britons' had long disappeared (hence the term 'Romano-Britons').

Carausius

The Saxon Shore forts were to play a significant role in the secession of Britannia – and part of northern Gaul – from the empire under the usurper Mausaeus Carausius, and in their reintegration into the empire by the Caesar, Constantius Chlorus, a decade later.

In late AD 285, Carausius, a Menapii by birth from the coastal region of Belgica, was commissioned to clear the sea of pirates: Aurelius Victor (*de Caesaribus* 39.20–21) mentions Saxones and Franci, while Eutropius (9.13, 21 cf. Orosius 7.25.3) calls them simply Germani. His command was described as covering the coasts of Belgica and Armorica, and would have certainly included the *classis Britannica*. He was clearly an experienced soldier with a thorough knowledge of the sea – it was said that in his youth he had served as a steersman – and an impressive record as a land commander, having recently suppressed a widespread revolt in Gaul. However, soon falling foul of the central administration, he proclaimed himself emperor of Britannia.

Once established in Britannia, with his Gallic command still intact, Carausius was in a strong position. Nonetheless, he extended his fleet by enlisting Gallic merchantmen and Frankish pirates (*Panegyrici Latini* VIII (5) 12.1). In the winter of AD 288, Maximian ordered a new fleet to be built on the Rhine and launched a seaborne assault on Britannia, but failed. Foul weather was blamed, but this probably obscures a defeat at the hands of Carausius or his allies (*Panegyrici Latini* X (2) 11.7, VIII (5) 12.1–2). There matters rested for four years, during which time Carausius consolidated his position. It was during this hiatus that Carausius attempted, through diplomacy and propaganda, to gain legitimacy for his rule. Coins minted by him attest this, one issue representing him as an equal

Gold medallion of Constantius Chlorus from Arras depicting the walls of London (*Londinium*). The spiritual personification of LON(dinium) kneels before the city gate to welcome Constantius, hailed as the 'restorer of external light' (*REDDITOR LVCIS AETERNAE*). Below is the fleet, the instrument of re-conquest. (Esther Carré)

colleague of Diocletianus and Maximian. Such brazen efforts to depict himself as the third member of their regime do not appear to have been reciprocated, and any possibility of a constitutional resolution was ended with the establishment of the Tetrarchy in AD 293.

The next attempt to oust Carausius was led by the newly appointed Caesar to Maximian, Constantius Chlorus. In a rapid thrust from the imperial stronghold at Trier (*Treveri*) he cleared Carausius' positions along the Gallic coast and took Boulogne-sur-Mer (*Gesoriacum Bononia*) (*Panegyrici Latini* VIII (5) 6.1–2), thus loosening Carausius' grip on the coastal region of northern Gaul. For Carausius this setback was fatal, and soon afterwards he was assassinated (it was said) by his finance officer, Allectus, who took over the role of emperor of Britannia (Eutropius 9.22.2). Over the next three years preparations were made to mount an invasion, with ships being built in the ports and estuaries of Gaul. Constantius eventually landed in Britannia and soundly defeated Allectus, who was killed during the fighting (*Panegyrici Latini* VIII (5) 6.14–20). The last separatist regime of the 3rd century AD had finally been brought to an end.

Barbarica conspiratio

Valentinianus I (r. AD 364–75) was on the road to Trier from Autun (Augustodunum) when news was brought to him of chaos in Britannia. The various barbarian peoples that had been harassing both Britannia and the north-western seaboard of Gaul had suddenly combined to organize a concerted attack, with the Picti, who are described by Ammianus as 'divided into two peoples, Dicalydonae and Verturiones' (27.8.5)[1], the Attacotti, and the Scotti assaulting Britannia, and the Franks and Saxons ravaging the coasts of Gaul. Such a *barbarica conspiratio* – barbarian conspiracy – was very rare.

In fact, if our reading of Ammianus is correct, this major incursion into the empire came by sea as well as land. One threat was from the Scotti of 'ice-bound Hibernia', and perhaps also from the Attacotti, an otherwise little-known people. Another was from the Picti from Caledonia. A third was from those sea-raiders the Roman historians call 'Saxones'[2], but who appear to have included contingents from several peoples along what is now the North Sea littoral, from Frisia, Saxony, and the Jutland peninsula.

The synchronized raids of AD 367 imply at least one very capable and well-informed military mind on the barbarian side. But they imply more besides, that is, a leader with the personal reputation and persuasiveness to weld such disparate peoples into a league to take a common action, if only for one operation.

In Britannia the *areani* or *arcani* (the reading is obscure) had progressively abandoned their duty, which was to gather intelligence and warn the Romans of likely trouble; Ammianus (28.3.8) tells us this in words that suggest a process that had been going on for some time. Seduced by offers of booty to come, they had allied themselves in secret to the *barbari* – barbarians – and, so we guess, passed information to them. This may lie behind one element of the disaster Valentinianus now learnt about. His *dux* Fullofaudes had been put out of action 'by the wiles of the enemy', either killed or pinned down somewhere, perhaps as he rushed from York-*Eboracum*. This was very serious indeed, seeing that Fullofaudes probably held the post later attested as *dux Britanniarum*, in command of the bulk of the static garrison of the island. A *dux* was a professional soldier who was primarily responsible for the protection of the sector of frontier assigned to him, and as part of this task he was to ensure that fortifications were built where necessary and the existing ones were kept in

---

[1] These peoples have such similar or even identical names to the Caledonii and Verturiones, peoples beyond Rome's northernmost frontier recorded by the Alexandrian geographer Ptolemaios (*Geographia* 2.3.8–12) in the mid-2nd century AD, that they are probably closely related.

[2] The Welsh and Irish terms for 'the English' remain to this day 'Saxons' (Welsh *Saeson*, Old Irish *Saxan*). Gildas (d. AD 570), like other writers in Latin, termed the Germanic settlers in Britain 'Saxones'. It is thus something of a puzzle why Pope Gregory the Great (AD 590–604) termed them English, a usage that prevailed.

The Arch of Galerius, Thessalonika, commemorates his success against the Persians in AD 298, and contains a number of reliefs depicting late Roman soldiers. Most wear scale body armour, helmets of the *spangenhelm* type, and carry large round or oval shields. (Author's collection)

good repair (e.g. *CT* 15.1.13). The *dux* also had charge of recruiting locally and assigning men to units under his command. Constantinus had insisted that *duces* should inspect all recruits who had already been approved, and weed out those who were unsuitable (*CT* 7.22.5).

Yet elimination of the *dux* was only part of the calamity reported to the emperor. Another of his generals had certainly been killed, this time an officer bearing the rank of *comes*; though the title itself was not specifically military in nature, nor did the possession of it imply that the owner held a specific post. However, if he was appointed to a specific post, his official title became *comes et ...* (count and ...). Thus smaller field forces, which had been detached from a field army (*comitatus*), usually came under the command of a *comes*. The *Notitia Dignitatum* (*Occ.* VII), for instance, later lists the *comes Britanniarum* as commanding six cavalry and three infantry units of the diocesan *comitatus*. Yet this particular commander, Nectaridus, is described as *comes maritimi tractus* – count of the maritime region. While it is likely that his command included the Saxon Shore forts, later listed in the *Notitia Dignitatum* under the *comes litoris Saxonici*, it is perfectly possible that in AD 367 he also commanded forts on the west coast, notably Cardiff and Lancaster.

The subsequent restoration of order by the *comes rei militaris* Flavius Theodosius, whose son was to become the emperor Theodosius I, included naval operations against Saxons, reminding us that the primary role of the Saxons and Franks in this enterprise was to harry Gaul rather than Britannia:

'Shall I relate how Britannia was brought to her knees by battles on land? In that case the Saxones, exhausted by naval engagements, spring to mind' (Pacatus *Panegyric on Theodosius* 5.2). Nectaridus' authority may well have covered both sides of the Oceanus Britannicus, and its overall scope may have been such as to require an officer of the rank of *comes*. It is possible, of course, that Nectaridus had been appointed to lead a task force specifically to clear out pirates, and it is interesting to note that Zosimus (4.35.5), when he mentions the events of this year, speaks of small raiding parties attacking Britannia. No matter, the loss of an officer of this rank would have been a serious blow to imperial prestige.

Stilicho

The death of Theodosius I left the empire to his two immature sons Arcadius and Honorius, both already invested with the rank of Augustus. It is the events of the reign of the younger of the two, Honorius (AD 395–423), that concern us here, and in particular those surrounding his Romano-Vandal generalissimo (*magister peditum praesentalis*), the remarkable Flavius Stilicho. Married to Theodosius' formidable niece (and adopted daughter) Serena, he had long been close to Theodosius and in the later years of his reign he had become the emperor's chief lieutenant. He was now *de facto* regent in the west, basing his authority on a claim that the dying emperor had secretly asked him to oversee his sons. Though never effective in the east, Stilicho's rule was for a decade more or less unchallengeable in the west. The dynastic connection of Stilicho and the imperial house was cemented by the marriage of his daughter Maria to the young Honorius.

The only contemporary source for Stilicho's policy towards Britannia is, unfortunately, the eulogizing court-poet Claudian. It is not therefore surprising that when he mentions these provinces it is in connection with claims of military success. However, it looks as if the imperial forces were able to assert control over the maritime approaches to the northwestern provinces in AD 398, including the defeat of both Saxon and Scotti. It is not clear whether the Picti, also mentioned as beaten, are included among the seaborne enemies or as a reference to a purely land campaign. With this remark of Claudian has been linked the second of the British chronicler-monk Gildas' so-called Pictish Wars. The latter reports an appeal for help from Britannia, to which the western government again responded by despatching an expedition against the enemy,

West face of marble plinth supporting the Obelisk of Karnak, Hippodrome, Istanbul. Enthroned in the imperial box, Theodosius I, flanked by his sons Arcadius (right) and Honorius (left), is awarding a charioteer a victory wreath. Honorius would go on to rule the western empire. (Author's collection)

this time 'against expectation'. If there is any thing behind that phrase, it may suggest that the barbarians, as in AD 367, were taking advantage of the fact that the imperial authorities were distracted by other affairs.

In the first half of AD 398 Stilicho had been involved in suppressing the potentially extremely damaging revolt led by Gildo, *comes Africae*, who had decided to assert allegiance to Arcadius and the eastern government on the issue of legitimacy. If anything was 'against expectation', it was the ease and speed with which Gildo was suppressed, leaving the western government free to turn to other problems, such as Britannia.

We do not know whether Stilicho personally took charge in the Britannic war. However, early in AD 400 the claims made in his honour are considerable. It is worth looking at Claudian's account in detail. After an introduction that depicts Britannia with the trappings of a Caledonian savage, she is made to declare:

> When I too was about to succumb to the attack of neighbouring peoples – for the Scotti have raised all Hibernia against me, and the sea foamed under hostile oars – you Stilicho, fortified me. This was to such effect that I longer do not fear the weapons of the Scotti, nor tremble at the Picti, nor along my shore do I look for the approaching Saxones on each uncertain wind. (*de consulatu Stilichonis* 2.247–55)

Without Stilicho's endeavours, a thankful Britannia is implying that she would have been the victim of seaborne attacks. It is difficult to see what was going on in Britannia because of his colourful style, but earlier in the year Claudian seems to have been expecting news of naval success, waiting to hear of 'the Saxones conquered, the Oceanus calmed, the Picti broken, and Britannia secure' (*In Eutropium* 1.392–93). Yet only a month after the detailed eulogy of January AD 400, the trumpeted claims of major success evaporate, and they do not reappear. Two years later Claudian gives us news of troop withdrawals from Britannia, but this seems too late to explain the change of tone in AD 400.

The eulogy of that year does not confirm victory in battle and concentrates on defence. Perhaps the best answer is that there was no actual victory, and that it was becoming obvious that Stilicho in fact had to run down the garrison of Britannia. It has been suggested that he was already abandoning forts at an early stage of his regency. Gildas may help us develop this idea. We have already seen that it would fit the general situation to have troops being withdrawn in AD 398. He goes on to say (*De excidio* 18.1) that just before the Romans left (after defeating the Picti in this 'second war'), they helped the Romano-Britons to build the stone wall, constructed watchtowers on the south coast, and provided patterns of weapons (*exemplaria armorum*) for the islanders. They then withdrew, and the Picti and Scotti occupied territory as far as Hadrian's Wall (*muro tenus*).

Faenza Mosaic from the Domus of via Dogana, early 5th century AD, Palazzo Mazzolani, Faenza. The scene shows Honorius (enthroned) and Stilicho (left foreground). Effectively regent of the west, Stilicho had inveigled himself into the Theodosian dynasty to rule through it, not in spite of it. (Author's collection)

Currachs

Gildas says (*De excidio* 19.1–2) the Picti and Scotti raided Britannia *de curucis*, which were black. This type of vessel was probably a currach. Of similar construction to the coracle, but much larger in size, the currach was a wooden- or wicker-framed vessel, covered with stitched and pitched animal hides, giving it its black appearance.

The construction of a currach is described in remarkable detail in the *Navigatio Sancti Brendani*: 'Brendan and his companions made a currach, using iron tools. The ribs and frames were of wood … and the covering was tanned ox-hide stretched over oak bark. They greased all the seams on the outer surface of the skin with fat and stored away spare skins inside the currach, together with forty days' supplies, fat for waterproofing the skins, tools and utensils' (4). Simple to construct using materials readily available and easily worked, the currach was the most extensively used type of vessel amongst the Picti and Scotti. Of deceptively strong construction and durability, the currach could carry a crew of several men. On his Atlantic voyage Brendan is said to have taken 17 fellow Irish monks with him. Hide-covered boats had the added advantage of being light, which meant the crew had the ability to carry or haul their ship overland. This added mobility could provide an added element of surprise in raiding.

The seagoing capability of the currach is demonstrated by reconstructions using traditional materials and techniques, notably by Tim Severin and his crew, who were able – in two seasons – to successfully cross the Atlantic. Currachs were propelled by both oars and sails, Gildas recording that the Picti and Scotti 'came relying on their oars as wings, on the arms of their oarsmen, and on the winds swelling their sails' (*De excidio* 16). And the *Navigatio Sancti Brendani* describes how 'a mast, a sail, and various pieces of equipment for steering were fitted into the vessel' (4). This mast was erected amidships. Severin's currach achieved rowing speeds of between 3 and 4 knots depending on the size of the oar crew. Performance under sail, however, was unimpressive. The average day's run was 40 nautical miles and a cruising speed of 2 to 3 knots was considered the norm in winds of Force 3 to 4 (Severin 1978: 289–90). The ultimate disadvantage to the currach is that the hide contributes nothing to the structural strength of the hull. This imposes a practical limit to the overall length, perhaps 18 to 20m, attainable with this method of construction (Grainge 2005: 72).

ABOVE Broighter boat (Dublin, National Museum of Ireland), which formed part of a hoard of superb Celtic gold found near Lough Foyle, County Derry. It is possible that the vessel modelled was a currach. The exquisitely made golden boat is complete with mast, steering-paddle, oarsmen's benches and oars. (Esther Carré)

By marrying the accounts of Gildas and Claudian we may conjecture the following scenario. The expedition sent out by Theodosius in AD 389 or AD 390 to deal with the 'first Pictish war' had become semi-permanent. There was a strong tendency for task forces of *comitatenses* to become localized, each under a *comes* as before but acquiring territorial titles, and the presence of a *comes Britanniarum* in the *Notitia Dignitatum* (*Occ.* XXIX, cf. VII) may well indicate such a situation occurring in Britannia at this time. In AD 398 it was being recalled, perhaps with consequent adjustments in the stationing of the garrison units in Britannia, including the evacuation of some less vital forts. The barbarians took the opportunity to attack, but were thrown off balance by the unexpected collapse of Gildo in Africa, and did not press home their attack. Finally, though the planned withdrawal was resumed, the warning was heeded, and measures were taken to strengthen the defences of the island. We do not have to assume the large-scale removal of garrison *limitanei*, as the fact that the barbarians stopped at Hadrian's Wall suggests the northern frontier held for the moment.

The provision of *exemplaria armorum*, and the instruction in the building of the stone wall are interesting. The first suggests the central authorities supplied patterns so that equipment normally supplied by the state ordnance factories could be manufactured locally. The latter, while in itself probably an attempt to

explain Hadrian's Wall when the truth about its construction had been lost, may preserve a tradition of deliberately instructing civilian builders in the techniques of military construction.

Among the troops collected by Stilicho for the Gothic wars, Claudian describes a *legio* (Gildas uses the same word, which is repeated again by Bede), 'protector of the furthest Britons, which curbs the ferocious Scotti and has watched the tattooed life draining from the dying Picti' (*Bellum Gothorum* 416–18). If Claudian could be trusted not to be using literary convention, this ought to mean part of the static garrison of northern Britannia – the most likely candidate being *legio VI Victrix* based at York-*Eboracum* – but it is just as likely that this is the same force that was being withdrawn at the time of Gildas' second Pictish war. We may perhaps guess that if this meant leaving the post of *comes Britanniarum* without a substantial body of troops, then there was occasion for a reorganization of the coastal defences of Britannia that fixed the Saxon Shore in the form in which it stands in the *Notitia Dignitatum*. It is not impossible that the very title *comes litoris Saxonici*, which does not appear anywhere earlier, owes its existence to Stilicho.

Reports from Irish annals of attacks on Britannia by the 'high king' of Hibernia, Niall of the Nine Hostages (Níall Nóigiallach), are perhaps to be associated with the year AD 405. According to tradition, it was then that Niall's sea-raiders took hostage one Succat, who is better known by his later name of St Patrick. Similarly, the *Gallic Chronicle*, written in AD 453, records that in AD 408 Britannia suffered a serious attack by Saxons. It looks as if Stilicho's previous work on the coastal system, conjectured above, was based on an accurate assessment of returning danger. Barbarian confidence was returning.

Constantinus

Britannia was evidently under military pressure in the last decades of the 4th century AD, and looked to the elevation of its own western emperor to solve the problem. The short and violent reign of Constantinus III (AD 407–11), first as *tyrannus* but then recognized in desperation by Honorius (Sozomen 9.11, Procopius *Wars* 3.2.31), was to be the last of a series of proclamations by the army in Britannia that began with Magnus Maximus (r. AD 383–88), the legendary Macsen Wledig of the Welsh folk tale of the same name in the *Mabinogion*.

By AD 409, Honorius' regime was crumbling, and his acceptance of Constantinus was an unsuccessful attempt to use Roman troops from Britannia to stabilize the worsening military situation in the west after the huge invasion of the Visigoths, Suevi and Alans that overran Gaul and entered Iberia. At this time the emperor's government, only just relocated to its final secluded refuge at Ravenna, had its hands full in Italy with Alaric and his Gothic confederation. The downfall and execution of Stilicho the previous summer had left Honorius with a vacuum in his military hierarchy. The western command was in fact directed from a cloistered ineffective court at Ravenna, which sheltered a personally weak emperor both from the invaders and from the realities outside his palace. Britannia, forever on the outside edge and now denuded of troops, was seriously threatened by 'the barbarians from over the Rhine' (Zosimus 6.5.2). With Constantinus' army bogged down in Iberia, the Romano-British *civitates*, who probably no longer believed that Constantinus might secure the diocese from external attack, expelled his officials and repelled the barbarians by themselves.

It is generally agreed that there had been a reduction of the garrison of Britannia, perhaps by as much as 40 to 50 per cent (Breeze 1984: 267–68). Both Zosimus (6.10.2) and Gildas refer to the 'rescript' of Honorius, a letter in which the emperor tells the Romano-British *civitates* that they should see to their own defence. That Honorius wrote to the *civitates* implies a transformation of the relationship between the empire and its citizens, for the *civitas* had been a central institution of civilian political life, while the central government had been responsible for the army. Honorius was, effectively, granting them independence from Rome. The Romano-British *civitates* thus had a choice: either hire defenders from among the barbarians or defend themselves.

For the most part the Romano-Britons took the second course of action, whereas their Romano-Gallic neighbours on the whole took the first. In Gaul an army of '12,000 Britanni' (Jordanes *Getica* 45.237, cf. Sidonius *Carmina* 3.9.1–2, Gregory of Tours *Historia Francorum* 2.18), under their king Riothamus, fought for the western empire against the Visigoths in AD 469. As part of Anthemius' anti-Gothic coalition it was intended to defend Aquitania Prima, but was betrayed by the praetorian prefect, Arvandus, and consequently defeated by the Visigoths of Euric (r. AD 466–84) at Bourg-de-Déols (*Vicus Dolensis*). The remnants of the army were driven to take refuge with the Burgundians, then in alliance with the empire.

According to Procopius, despite the death of Constantinus and his two sons in battle, the 'Romans never succeeded in recovering Britannia, but it remained from that time on under tyrants' (*Wars* 3.2.38). Indeed, archaeology bears out the view that Britannia, or Britain as we should now call it, became detached from the empire in the early 5th century AD, whatever sentiments lingered among some Romano-Britons. For instance, the importation of fresh imperial coinage into Britain appears to have ceased after the reign of Constantinus, implying both a disconnection from the imperial payment of troops and the imperial taxation system.

Design

During the late 3rd century AD Roman defensive architecture as a whole was in a state of change. New defences – both military and urban – were built on an altogether massive scale. Curtains became thicker and higher than had previously been the norm, and increases in scale were accompanied by architectural innovations. Solid, forward-projecting towers were built at intervals around the new defensive circuits, thus providing firing platforms for archers or artillery. Gateways, of course, were potential weak points. They too became more heavily defended, often with flanking towers or towers on either side of a single, narrow entranceway.

Exemplifying the move to a different type of warfare in which massive, freestanding walls and forward-projecting towers were of overwhelming importance, these military installations exhibit brutal functionalism. In terms of design the old-style forts of the Principate had been sited aggressively to control movement, with towers that projected above their ramparts for observation and to impress tribal peoples, not beyond them for enfilading fire. The army of the early empire trained to meet its opponents in the field; in the late empire this role was reserved for the *comitatenses*, most of whom were stationed well within the provinces. Direct attack on a military installation was now a real possibility, and the army was no longer quite so confident about advancing to destroy the enemy in the open.

There are, of course, variations in design directed to the same end: thus towers almost invariably project from the curtain, but they may be round, semicircular, D-shaped, fan-shaped, polygonal, or rectangular. It was the tactic of individual installations to keep assailants as far away as possible. New forts

South wall of the defences and west guard-chamber of the south gate of the fort at Caister-on-Sea. Constructed from local flint cobbles and other beach stone, the narrow, rectangular-profiled wall was backed by a sizeable earthen bank. (Author's collection)

were sited on elevated ground, preferably a plateau even if its irregular outline imposed the same outline on the defences. The narrow V-shaped cross-section ditches of the Principate were superseded by wide, flat-bottomed ditches, flooded if possible, set further from the walls so as to create a 'killing zone'. These walls now required a wider berm for stability: they were not the stone-revetted earthen embankments of the early empire, but thick curtain walls of concrete rubble faced with masonry. The use of salvaged material is common, including monumental sculptures and tombstones. Alternatively, many installations were simply brought up to date by repairing the existing defences and perhaps modernizing them.

Construction methods

When considering the forts of the Wash–Solent *limes* the method of construction was, in all cases, broadly similar. The building process began with the excavation of a roughly vertical-sided, flat-bottomed trench, ranging from 0.7 to 1.5m between sites. The main constituents of the foundations were 'dry' materials, such as flint, chalk or other locally available stones, and occasionally clay. Thin spreads of concrete could be employed (Brancaster, Pevensey). Where the subsoil was considered to be unstable, or the walls were to be built to a considerable height, timber piles were driven several metres into the base of the trench to provide additional underpinning (Richborough, Lympne, Pevensey).

Construction of the superstructure began at, or a little below, the contemporary ground level. The lowest component was normally a plinth of large blocks, wider than the masonry above, and stepped out on one or both faces. Above the plinth the outer face was vertical, but in many instances the inner face was tapered (Burgh Castle), or progressively thinned by a series of offsets (Pevensey), thus creating a more stable structure.

A course of small, neat cubes (*petit appareil*) of split flint was laid to form the inner and outer face of the wall, creating a trough that was then in-filled with a mixture of rubble and mortar (sand, beach pebbles, lime), which was then compressed by ramming. The next course of facing stones was then laid, and the process repeated. Once the wall reached heights of around 1.5m and above, scaffolding became necessary. This was timber framed and supported either on horizontal poles that ran right through the wall-core, or by a series of short horizontal poles linked to the walls by tie-beams and thus providing a framework on which planks were laid.

The total height of defences is not known for certain. Vitruvius, writing in the time of Augustus, had recommended that the rampart-walk should 'be so made that armed men meeting one another … can pass without hindrance' (1.5.1), thus the thickness of the highest surviving section of wall at Burgh Castle (4.5m) suggests that here the defences stand close to their full height. Adding a parapet of 1.6m suggests that the complete height of the defences was around 6m. Other forts had wider, taller defences (Richborough, Pevensey, Portchester).

There was a potential weakness in such a construction method, namely at the junction of the shallow facing stones and the rubble-mortar core. Although builders often used material for their facing that had a long tail that could be well held by the wall mortar, as an extra security, one or several horizontal bonding courses were also used at regular vertical intervals. The material used in these courses was normally deep flat stones, bricks or reused tiles. These reached further back into the wall-core than the facing stones themselves, and helped to key in the facing more securely. Bonding courses, a minor but nonetheless significant change in defensive architecture, also served as a means of levelling the wall during construction.

Raw materials

The raw materials for building the Saxon Shore forts were drawn from far and near, but in most cases local supply was the dominant factor.

Lympne was the most compact project in this respect, for here the Roman builders had virtually all their materials immediately to hand. Limestone from an outcrop within a few hundred metres of the building site was used for the core rubble and the facing stones, and was also burnt to produce lime for the mortar. Sand and pebbles were procured from the beach at the base of the slope below the site, while the small quantities of timber needed could also have been felled locally. Much of the brick and tile in the bonding courses had been recycled from earlier structures.

Reculver, on the other hand, is perhaps more typical of the project as a whole. For here nearly 90 per cent of the enceinte was built using materials probably procured within 20km of the site. In this instance the only stone to

South wall of Burgh Castle-*Gariannum*, a close-up view showing the construction. Brick bonding courses usually provided horizontal stability by running from the facing into the centre of the core. However, here at Burgh Castle they are only surface deep. (Author's collection)

travel any distance was Kentish ragstone, for use as facing material, from the Medway quarries some 70km away (Pearson 2002: 79).

Reused building materials were an important source. The recycling of materials can be best seen at Richborough and Lympne, where old *tegulae* roofing tiles were incorporated into the bonding courses. Though generally hard to detect, reused stone can be seen also at these two sites, where second-hand monumental blocks formed part of the foundations. In fact, at Richborough it seems that up to 70 per cent of the raw materials needed to construct the defences probably came from the 'Great Monument', which incorporated some 16,000m^3 of flint, tufa and marble (Pearson 2002: 80).

In most cases it was the seashore that provided the vast majority of stone for the defences. Exploitation of unconsolidated deposits was of prime importance, with beach stone, flint especially, being widely used. Sand and pebbles for the mortar was also procured from beaches.

Human resources

Most building tasks did not require skilled workers as the majority of the labour was absorbed by the quarrying process and tasks such as the intra-site movement of raw materials. Thus only a small percentage of the workforce needed to be skilled craftsmen, for example masons and sawyers, while the remainder of the men on site were simply needed to carry out the basic physical tasks.

Obviously the Roman Army played a central role in the construction of the Saxon Shore forts, though additional manpower could have been drawn from the local civilian population, particularly skilled artisans. In addition to providing a valuable pool of ready labour, the army also possessed within its ranks a significant number of skilled craftsmen. The 2nd-century jurist Tarrutienus Paternus, the praetorian prefect under Commodus (r. AD 180–92) and a respected military jurist, makes this clear. His list of those soldiers exempt from normal duties (*immunes*) included specialists such as 'architects … shipwrights … cartwrights … stone-cutters, men who burn lime, men who cut wood, and men who chop and burn charcoal' (*Digesta* 50.6.7). Here, evidently, is the complete list of skills necessary to build the forts, from construction of transportation, through quarrying, to the actual process of building.

From the early dated forts of Reculver-*Regulbium* and Brancaster-*Branoduno* we have the stamped tiles of *cohors I Baetasiorum* and *cohors I Aquitanorum* respectively, which provide direct evidence for the involvement of these units in the construction of these installations. In fact, before its move south, *cohors I Aquitanorum* had been stationed at Brough-on-Noe, where it had recently been engaged in building work (*RIB* 283).

West wall of Richborough-*Rutupiae*; a close-up showing the construction. Two courses of large stone blocks form the plinth, above which is the exposed rubble core of chalk, flint and septaria. Higher up the small facing stones remain in situ, bonded to the core by brick bonding courses. The square holes would have held the scaffolding. (Esther Carré)

Curtain walls

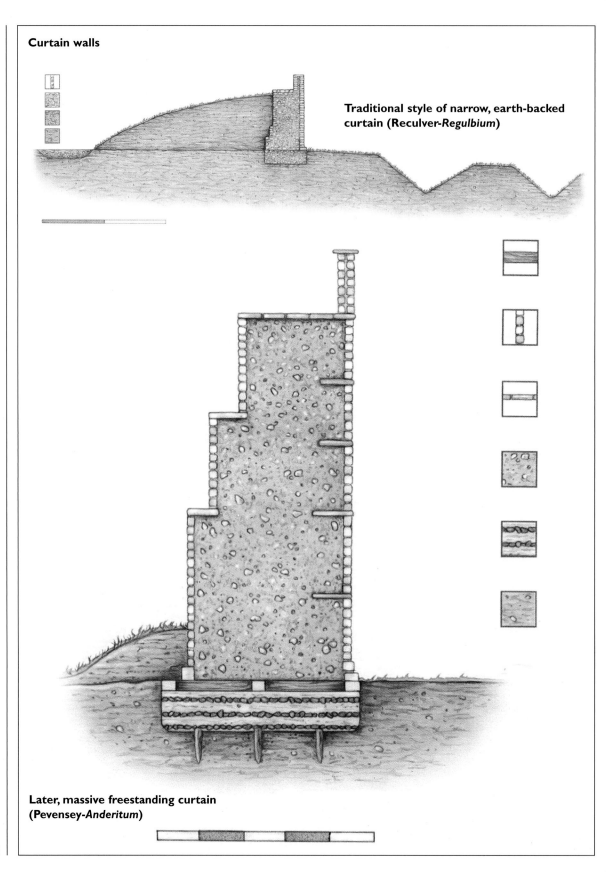

Traditional style of narrow, earth-backed curtain (Reculver-*Regulbium*)

Later, massive freestanding curtain (Pevensey-*Anderitum*)

Curtain walls

Defence, in the Principate, meant aggressive response or even offensive pre-emptive strikes into enemy territory before there could be any attack on Roman installations. The defences provided were sufficient to repel a sudden raid, but were not designed to withstand a prolonged siege. Towards the end of the 3rd century AD, however, offensive defence was not always possible, and this is clearly reflected in fortification designs that represent a radical departure from simple defences of the preceding centuries.

Traditional style of narrow, earth-backed curtain (Reculver-*Regulbium*)

The combination of stone curtain and earthen bank had been the product of the military architecture of the turn of the 2nd century AD. The foundations consist of a trench filled entirely with small flint cobbles. The curtain is 3m at the base and reduces by two internal offsets to 2.4m. It has a flint-rubble core, and an outer facing of neatly squared blocks of Kentish ragstone. Behind the curtain is a sloping bank of clay and earth, built largely from material obtained when the two external ditches were dug, some 15m wide. This provides a substantial back for the curtain and gives the defenders access to the rampart-walk.

Later, massive freestanding curtain (Pevensey-*Anderitum*)

The foundations at Pevensey-*Anderitum* are pretty elaborate. Above vertical piles driven deep into the trench base, successive layers of flint and crushed chalk have been laid down and rammed. Resting on the top chalk layer, just below ground level, is a lattice of large timber baulks. Chalk has been packed in the spaces between the timbers and a layer of mortar spread over the top, sealing the foundations and ensuring a level platform for the superstructure. The curtain, of sandstone blocks pointed with a strong pink mortar containing an aggregate of crushed brick, has horizontal bonding courses of brick and sandstone slabs at intervals. The core is comprised mainly of flint. A small earthen bank extends a short distance up the curtain's inner face.

For the later group of Saxon Shore forts the situation becomes somewhat less clear. As the 3rd century AD progressed the army presence in Britannia was greatly reduced, such that by the end of the century the number of troops is likely to have been more than half of the estimated 55,000 troops present in AD 210 (Breeze 1984: 267). Crucially, the composition of the army had also changed during the course of the century. In absolute numbers, therefore, and terms of the available skilled craftsmen, the army can be seen to be a much-reduced resource after the middle of the 3rd century AD. Despite these reductions, however, the army in Britannia may not have been overstretched, and the province was largely unscathed by the upheavals elsewhere in the empire. It is quite plausible that the army provided the whole workforce, and any troops introduced from Gaul during the supremacy of Carausius and Allectus would have boosted the potential labour force.

North wall of the fort at Richborough-*Rutupiae*. These massive walls were faced with rows of square stones separated at intervals by brick bonding courses. The use of chalk and ironstone ashlar blocks in this wall has provided it with a chequerboard pattern. (Leo Fields)

Anatomy

The notion of the Wash–Solent *limes* as a single system maintained as a unity throughout the life of individual forts does not survive examination of the dating evidence. The dating of the construction of individual forts depends in part on coin finds and in part on typology, and on the strength of this evidence it appears the late forts were built over several decades, starting with Burgh Castle-*Gariannum* and ending with Pevensey-*Anderitum*.

Moreover, it is possible to detach from the late-3rd century AD context three of the named series, that is Brancaster-*Branoduno*, Caister-on-Sea and Reculver-*Regulbium*. As examples of military architecture in Romano-Britain, they were all in the style of the 2nd century AD. In plan the defences were rectangular and round cornered. Their curtains were narrow – stone built but without bonding courses – and backed by a broad earthen bank that extended to the rampart-walk. Internal turrets were present at some or all of the angles, while gateways, one in each side of the fort, tended to be relatively simple in their design and only lightly defended. This is in direct line with the tradition of the turf and timber forts and their immediate stone successors (Fields 2003: 6, 16–20).

Built somewhat later than the first group of Saxon Shore forts, Burgh Castle-*Gariannum* can be seen as displaying transitional characteristics in the architecture of its defences. Its forward-projecting, curvilinear (better described as 'pear-shaped') towers are only bonded to the upper levels of the curtains, suggesting that they may have been an addition to the original structure, while the corner towers are rendered somewhat ineffective by the fort's rounded corners. Such a curious transitional arrangement would have had the effect of restricting the corner towers' field of fire, as they do not project far enough beyond the line of the walls.

The inner ditch, southern defences, Caister-on-Sea, averages 3m in depth along its length. Albeit only acting as an obstacle, any attacker climbing from its steep sides would not be able to use his shield, making him more vulnerable to missile fire from the walls. (Author's collection)

This fort was obviously begun in the style of 2nd-century military architecture, with rounded corners, but completed in the newly evolving defensive style with forward-projecting towers. Dover-*Dubris* also imperfectly incorporates forward-projection towers and might be dated to the period AD 275–80 (Wilkinson 1994: 72–73), as can Lympne-*Lemanis* (Pearson 2002: 59). Bradwell-*Othona* is not closely dated, but would appear on coin evidence to have been built around the same time.

Richborough-*Rutupiae* has been dated to the early AD 270s, but numerous coins of Carausius found in the lowest occupation levels of the fort suggests that it may have been constructed at any time at the beginning of his reign, AD 285 or soon after. The dating evidence for the construction of Portchester-*Portus Adurni*, in particular a coin of Carausius, points to a *terminus post quem* for its construction in the mid AD 280s and makes it credible that Carausius can be credited with its construction (Cunliffe 1975A: 60). Recent work at Pevensey-*Anderitum* dates the fort firmly to the reign of Allectus, AD 293 or shortly thereafter (Fulford-Tyers 1995).

Defences

As already noted, the dominant features in the new mode of defensive architecture were broad, high curtains, massive

forward-projecting towers, single entranceways flanked by strong towers and, usually, a broad ditch or ditches surrounding the whole work. However, the Saxon Shore forts were products of their time in which new and old elements mingled together, in some cases in the same enceinte.

Brancaster-*Branoduno*

Little trace of the Saxon Shore fort at Brancaster-*Branoduno* remains above ground apart from a slight hint of the platform it previously stood upon. Moreover the once highly irregular, indented coastline has changed considerably, and in Roman times the fort was at the head of a sheltered natural harbour. This haven has been long lost, the process of silting having left it a shadow of its former self.

The defences were virtually square in plan, with rounded corners, internal angle-turrets and backed by a substantial earthen bank. The curtains were of stone (possibly local flint cobbles), 2.9m wide and enclosed an area of 2.89ha (7.14 acres). Only a single shallow, V-shaped ditch surrounded the fort.

Caister-on-Sea

Again the coastline has changed considerably since Roman times, and Caister-on-Sea was then at the mouth of a large estuary stretching some way inland; where Great Yarmouth now lies was sea. The Roman site was originally interpreted as a small harbour town founded probably in the second half of the 2nd century AD, but the presence of stone walls belonging to the early 3rd century AD, unparalleled for a town at such an early date, and its similarity with the earliest forts of the Saxon Shore system, prompted the re-interpretation of the

Site of the fort at Brancaster-*Branoduno*, looking north-west across the plateau. Robbing of the fort's defences had already begun by the medieval period, evidence of which can be seen in the nearby Brancaster parish church. (Author's collection)

Gateways and towers

**Portchester-*Portus Adurni*
(Watergate)**

**Pevensey-*Anderitum*
(west gate)**

site as a fort. At London-*Londinium*, for instance, the riverside defences were not erected until AD 294, either by Allectus in preparation for the imperial attack or by Constantius Chlorus soon after.

The defences at Caister-on-Sea were slightly off square with rounded corners and backed by an earthen bank. The curtains were constructed using local flint cobbles and other beach stone, 2.9m wide, and enclosed an area of 2.62ha (6.47 acres). Two V-shaped ditches surrounded the fort, the outer one of which was substantially widened at some stage, probably during the early 4th century AD.

The forts at Caister-on-Sea and Burgh Castle faced one another across the 'Great Estuary', a major tidal inlet that opened to the sea in the area now occupied by Great Yarmouth. This view looks north-north-west from the south wall of the fort at Burgh Castle-*Gariannum* towards Caister-on-Sea. (Leo Fields)

OPPOSITE
Gateways and towers

With the new trend in fortifications massive towers, usually solid enough to support light artillery, now strengthened the defences. These were forward projecting in order to gain distance from the curtains so as to afford a better view of the defences and prevent anyone from approaching too closely by enfilading fire.

Towers, above the level of the rampart-walk, had two chambers each normally provided with large windows with semicircular arches. Wide openings are consonant with the use of artillery (*ballistae*), which to be effective needs a wide arc of fire. *Ballistae* were light spring guns that fired bolts (*iacula*), and their size would indicate that several could be mounted in a single tower (Ammianus 23.4.2–3, Anonymous *De rebus bellicis* 18.1–5, Vegetius *Epit.* 4.22, Procopius *Wars* 1.21.14–18). These twin-armed torsion machines had a range of some 400m, and therefore, if used carefully, could keep an enemy from coming in close to the defences. Anecdotes of near misses in Ammianus (19.1.5, 7, cf. 5.6, 7.4) confirm that the *ballista* was an effective anti-personnel weapon. To support the added weight of these machines and their three-man crews, towers were usually of solid masonry below the level of the rampart-walk. Roofs were either flat and crenellated, or covered with a conical roof of tiles, the former providing another fighting platform.

Gateways, also, were massively built, and hemmed in by a pair of thick-walled, usually U-shaped, towers. These would cover the approaches to the gate as well as enfilading the adjacent curtains. The gate itself sat at the rear of this passage, to allow the defenders to interdict the immediate approaches, and was made of hard wood,

covered in iron plates to protect it against burning. Gateways were all constructed with a two-storied curtain pierced by a single entranceway, but otherwise varied in design according to the relative importance of each.

Portchester-*Portus Adurni* (Watergate)
The Watergate has a single portal set at the back of a courtyard, 13.75m wide and 11m deep, in an in-turn of the enceinte. This is a rather rare style of gateway in the late Roman world, and is almost a throwback to the Augustan idea of a monumental courtyard in front of the gate. It manages to enfilade the entranceway without breaking the symmetry of the forward-projecting, curvilinear towers on the seaward side of the fort. A pair of square guard-chambers flanks the 3m-wide gate. The walls are of rubble concrete, with a facing of split flint and bonding courses of flat stone. The Landgate of the east side is of the same design, while simple posterns pierce the north and south walls.

Pevensey-*Anderitum* (west gate)
This gateway is a developed form of the Watergate. It consists of a central arched entranceway 2.75m wide, with two guard-chambers on either side. The entranceway is set behind the line of the walls, and two gigantic, U-shaped towers flank the whole structure. This defensive arrangement allowed the area in front of the entranceway to be commanded by fire from three sides. To the front of the gateway is a V-shaped ditch that cuts across the isthmus joining the peninsula on which the fort stands to the mainland. The walls are of sandstone blocks, with bonding courses of brick and sandstone slabs. The core is mainly of flint.

The fort at Burgh Castle-*Gariannum* is in a fine state of preservation. This view looking west shows the flint-faced and predominately flint-cored east wall, which still stands to almost its original height. (Author's collection)

Burgh Castle-*Gariannum*

The Roman name *Gariannum* probably means 'babbling river', the river being the Yare on which the Saxon Shore fort stands. The fort lies only a short distance from Caister-on-Sea, but in Roman times the two installations lay on opposite sides of a large estuary. It is a curious transitional structure, begun in the style of a typical 2nd-century fort, with rounded corners and internal turrets, but completed in the later manner with forward-projecting towers.

The flint-faced and predominantly flint-cored defences stood to heights above 4m. The inner faces are not vertical, but taper as they rise. This innovation allowed the curtains to be freestanding, thus making an earthen bank unnecessary. Triple bonding courses of brick were employed at close vertical intervals on exterior faces, tying the shallow, split-flint facings more securely to their cores. The width of the curtains varied around the circuit. The west wall and western portions of the north and south walls were 2.2m thick, while the heavier east wall, built on more level ground, was 3.2m wide. In place of a regular

South wall of Burgh Castle-*Gariannum*, part standing, part toppling, part fallen. The standing section retains all its facing-flints, separated by rows of brick bonding courses, 3.2m thick at base and 4.5m high – probably its original height except for a parapet. (Author's collection)

shape, the defences had a trapezoidal quadrilateral plan with rounded corners, encompassing an area of 2.4ha (5.9 acres). Ten forward-projecting, curvilinear towers studded the circuit at fairly regular intervals.

Walton Castle

A series of sketches exist of the fort before its total destruction by coastal erosion. This drawing, thought to be an early 18th-century copy of an original dating to 1623, shows a plan somewhat similar to Burgh Castle-*Gariannum*. Forward-projecting, curvilinear towers are present at the corners of the fort. Split-flint facing and brick bonding courses are also depicted, which corresponds to a 1722 description by a certain Dr Knight, in which he says the fort is 'composed of Pepple [pebbles/cobble] and Roman bricks in three courses' (quoted in Pearson 2002: 20). The presence of forward-projecting towers and rounded corners is good evidence for a construction date contemporary to other forts such as Burgh Castle-*Gariannum* and Bradwell-*Othona*.

Bradwell-*Othona*

The site of the Saxon Shore fort at Bradwell-*Othona* encompasses an unparalleled view of the entrances to the Blackwater and the Colne, the latter river leading

Richborough-*Rutupiae*

The Saxon Shore fort at Richborough-*Rutupiae* was built at the end of a small peninsula inside the southern entrance to the Wantsum, which then still separated the Isle of Thanet from mainland Kent. The Wantsum was a large tidal channel that provided a safe passage for ships seeking access to the Thames-*Tamesis* and London-*Londinium* from the *Oceanus Britannicus*, avoiding the risks of tacking round Thanet.

The fort was thus ideally positioned in a sheltered, tidal environment that lay close to the open sea.

The fort is equipped with thick, freestanding walls, projecting towers at regular intervals, and narrow, heavily defended entrances. Two deep V-shaped ditches augment these defences. The interior is not crammed with buildings like forts of the 1st and 2nd centuries AD. The only masonry structure is a modest bathhouse. Timber buildings are placed against and under the lee of

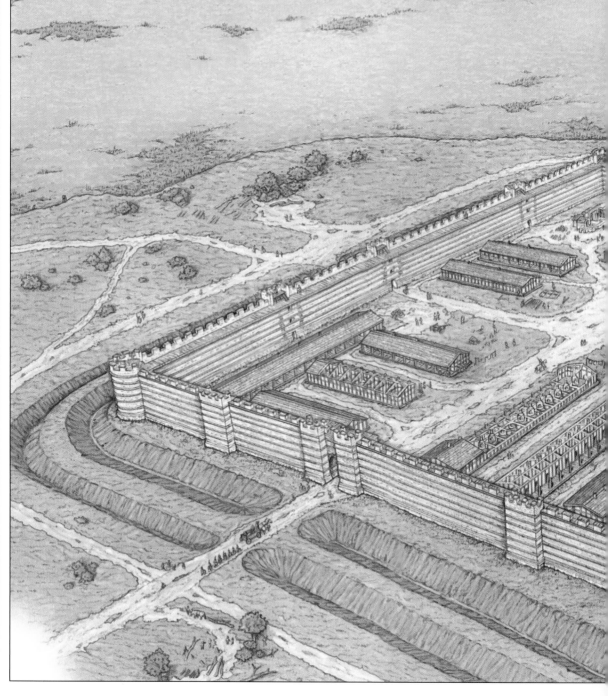

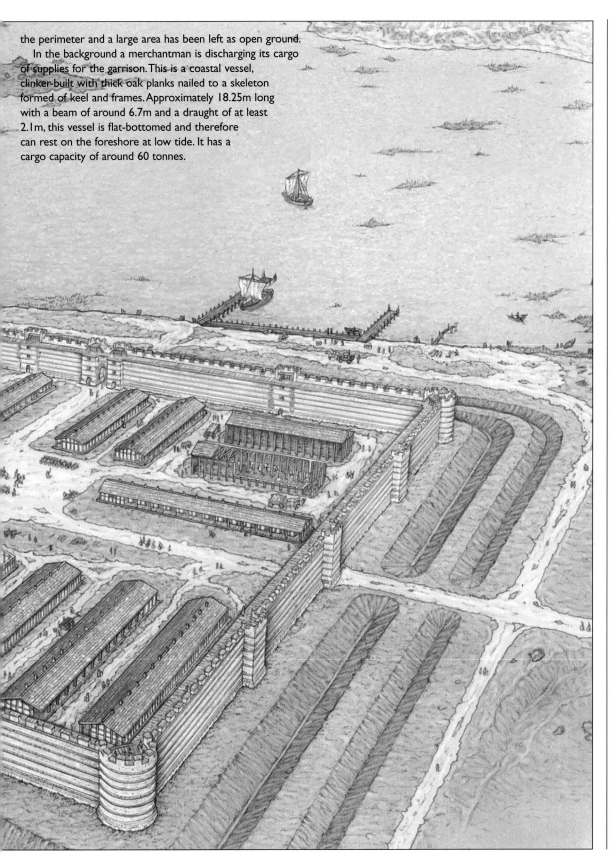

the perimeter and a large area has been left as open ground.
    In the background a merchantman is discharging its cargo of supplies for the garrison. This is a coastal vessel, clinker-built with thick oak planks nailed to a skeleton formed of keel and frames. Approximately 18.25m long with a beam of around 6.7m and a draught of at least 2.1m, this vessel is flat-bottomed and therefore can rest on the foreshore at low tide. It has a cargo capacity of around 60 tonnes.

to the important Roman town of Colchester-*Camulodunum*. It is not difficult to imagine the relative ease with which raiders could be observed as soon as they entered one of the estuaries, to be intercepted, at least when they returned from their business ashore.

Only the mid-7th century Saxon chapel of St Peter, which occupies the location of the fort's west gate, now marks the Roman site. Much Roman material is evident in the chapel, which is predominantly built of reused brick and limestone ashlar. Nevertheless, the defences survived at least until the seventeenth century, and were described as a 'huge ruin' by Philemon Holland in his edition of William Camden's *Britannia* (1637: 443). Later excavations established the trapezoidal plan of the defences, which survive on the northern, southern and western sides, and it seems the fort had rounded corners similar to Burgh Castle-*Gariannum*.

The surviving curtains enclose an area of 2ha (4.9 acres), and the whole fort was doubtless rather larger. A forward-projecting, curvilinear tower was found in the north-west corner, and also an interval tower between this corner and the chapel. The curtains were constructed using local septarian cementstones. Triple bonding courses of brick were employed at close vertical intervals on exterior faces. A section cut across the line of the south wall showed it to be 4.2m thick, indicating a tall, substantial superstructure. Beyond the defences was a single V-shaped ditch.

Reculver-*Regulbium*

Here too the coastline has changed dramatically and the present marine landscape at Reculver bears little resemblance to Roman *Regulbium* or 'great headland'. The main differences lie in the interchange between land and sea. In Roman times the Isle of Thanet was a complete island, separated from the mainland by a tidal channel, the Wantsum. Reculver-*Regulbium* guarded the

The north wall of Richborough-*Rutupiae*, which was high enough to stop attackers from climbing it unaided, necessitating the use of scaling ladders. This forward-projecting, rectangular tower defends the north postern. By projecting from the curtain, the tower allowed enfilading fire. (Leo Fields)

northern entry into the channel, but it was probably about 1.5km inland from the open sea to the north. Reculver itself sits on Thanet Beds, mostly made up of soft sands and clays, and it is these that have eroded so quickly. The land north of Reculver has been entirely removed by massive erosion and indeed even half of the fort itself has been swept into the sea.

The defences are of the 'traditional' style, as befits their construction date in the early 3rd century AD. This dating is supported by a building inscription referring to a certain Rufinus, perhaps the Q. Aradius Rufinus who was governor of Britannia Superior *c*. AD 240. A substantial earthen bank backed the relatively narrow curtains, 3m wide at the base and reduced by two internal offsets to 2.4m. These were built, without bonding courses, of local Kentish ragstone with a flint-rubble core, and originally enclosed an area of some 3.06ha (7.56 acres). A single, internal angle-turret has been found in the south-west corner. Two V-shaped ditches surrounded the fort.

Richborough-*Rutupiae*

The Saxon Shore fort at Richborough-*Rutupiae* guarded the southern entry to the Wantsum channel in a sheltered position with easy access to the Oceanus Britannicus and the Roman port at Dover-*Dubris*. Extensive silting over the centuries has now blocked the Roman channel and only the marshland and dykes now mark the place where Roman shipping once sailed. These environmental changes have left the Roman fort high and dry some 3km from the open sea.

Although a little smaller in area than the neighbouring fort at Reculver-*Regulbium* (2.5ha, 6 acres), the defences of the fort at Richborough-*Rutupiae* seem to have been significantly more substantial, and were certainly more architecturally advanced. The curtains, 3.3m wide at the base, still survive to heights above 8m. These were built predominantly of split flint, with a variety of other, mostly local, materials employed in the facing.

The north wall was constructed in large part using stone from the demolished triumphal arch, the so-called Great Monument. Double bonding courses of brick (and a little reused tile) are present at vertical intervals of around 1m. Forward-projecting towers studded the circuit. At the corners these massive structures were round and solid, while those in the intervals between the corners and the gateways were rectangular and hollow. Two V-shaped ditches augmented the defences.

LEFT Interval tower, east wall of Burgh Castle-*Gariannum*. Its construction technique is very similar to that of the curtain, but it is not bonded in with it for the first 2.4m of its height. This suggests it was an addition to the construction work after it had begun, though at an early stage. (Author's collection)

CENTRE Rampart-walk, east wall of Burgh Castle-*Gariannum*, looking south towards the south-east tower. Note the rounded corner immediately behind the forward-projecting tower, a good example of new and old elements mingled together in the same circuit. (Author's collection)

RIGHT The forward-projecting towers, east wall of Burgh Castle-*Gariannum*, were probably designed with the deployment of artillery, especially *ballistae*, in mind. The solid construction of these towers, coupled with their close positioning and good fields of fire, supports this view. (Author's collection)

Dover-*Dubris*

Whereas many natural havens have been lost, either left far inland or represented by shadows of their former selves, others, such as Dover-*Dubris*, owe their continued existence to their economic importance. Consequently the Saxon Shore fort, like the two bases of the *classis Britannica* that preceded it, now lies under the busy town centre of Dover and is known only from rescue archaeology.

Due to limited excavation work, the plan of the whole site is a little uncertain, though a completely rectangular shape is ruled out because the south and west walls meet at an angle greater than 90 degrees. Where excavated, the curtains have been found in very good condition. Built mainly of chalk and tufa (probably reused from the 2nd-century *classis Britannica* fort), 2.3 to 2.6m thick and backed by an earthen bank, these narrow curtains survive to heights of 4.5m. Apart from a slight step-in at ground level on the exterior face, they appear to have risen to their full height without offsets.

In total six forward-projecting, curvilinear towers have been excavated, spaced at slightly irregular intervals of between 23 to 30m. Two tower types have been identified, some built as an integral part of the curtains and others added at a later stage – though quite possibly during the main construction phase of the fort – as if it was realized that the spacing between the original towers was too great. The building materials also differ between these two types: the integral towers are constructed from chalk and tufa, while the added towers have a split-flint facing that employs brick bonding courses. Beyond the defences was a broad, V-shaped ditch.

Lympne-*Lemanis*

The Saxon Shore fort at Lympne-*Lemanis* stands on a scarp edge overlooking the extensive levels that now make up Romney Marsh and run south-eastwards towards Dungeness Point. The morphology was very different in the Roman period. The so-called Isle of Oxney was originally an area of creeks and inlets

The foundations of the north-west tower, west wall of Richborough-*Rutupiae*. Unlike the rectangular interval towers, this curvilinear tower was solid masonry up to the level of the rampart-walk, as were the other three corner towers. (Leo Fields)

at a point where at least three river systems eventually combined to form a tidal bay, which extended east-north-east towards Hythe. This in turn explains the position of the fort. It controlled a small harbour created by a southward spur at Lympne, at the entrance to this strategic estuary.

The destruction of the fort has led to considerable confusion as to its original plan. Not only has the south wall completely disappeared above ground level, but also it seems none of the remaining masonry is in its original location. Recent reconstructions envisage the fort as an irregular pentagon, with an angle mid-way along the north wall, covering an area of some 3.4ha (8.4 acres).

The surviving portions of the north, west and east walls indicate that the enceinte was very substantial, and also of advanced design. In places the walls still stand 6m tall and 3.9m thick at Roman ground level, studded with forward-projecting curvilinear towers, of which originally there were probably around 14. There is a very considerable quantity of reused material in the curtains, perhaps taken from an earlier nearby Roman installation. Many *tegulae* roofing tiles are evident in the bonding courses and the large stone slabs in the foundation of the east gate tower are also recycled material.

Watling Street crossing the double ditches of Richborough-*Rutupiae*. Beyond is the west gate of the fort, which was defended by a guard-chamber on either side (south one still visible) of its single entranceway. (Leo Fields)

Pevensey-*Anderitum*

This Saxon Shore fort, too, now lies inland. In Roman times the defences were built on a peninsula, with the sea coming right up to the south curtain and the harbour. The Roman name for Pevensey was *Anderitum*, meaning 'the great ford'.

The irregular oval plan of the defences, atypical of Roman military construction as a whole, can be explained by the need to fit the fort to the end of the peninsula on which it was built. Occupying an area of 3.65ha (9 acres), this is the largest of the Saxon Shore forts. The curtains still stand to over 8m high, are 4.2m in width at the base, and are thinned by a series of internal offsets to 2.4m. The facing was composed of sandstone blocks, with bonding courses of brick and sandstone slabs. The core was composed mainly of flint. A small earthen bank was present, extending a short distance up the inner face of each curtain.

The walls were strengthened by at least 13 solid, forward-projecting, curvilinear towers, placed at irregular intervals around the circuit. Three gateways are known: a heavily defended west gate, a less elaborate east gate, and a narrow north postern. The existence of at least one more entrance, somewhere along the lost south wall, seems likely.

Portchester-*Portus Adurni*

Unlike many of the Saxon Shore forts, the marine landscape has changed little here over the centuries, and the on the east side the water still laps up to the walls as it did in Roman times. The Roman name is uncertain, but most agree that it is probably *Portus Adurni* listed in the *Notitia Dignitatum*, although the particular form of the name recorded there may be corrupted.

The fort took the form of a regularly planned square enclosing an area 3.43ha (8.48 acres), surrounded by two V-shaped ditches. There were 20 forward-projecting, curvilinear towers originally: 14 now remain, at present hollow, but possibly originally solid. Four centrally placed gateways pierced the enceinte, those on the east (Landgate) and west (Watergate) being protected by substantial inset guard-chambers, while those on the north and south were simple posterns. As at Pevensey-*Anderitum*, whose defences it resembles, the curtains here were substantial. Surviving to a height of around 6m, they are 3.8m wide at the base. The facing was of split flint, as is the core, with bonding courses of flat stone set deep into the walls.

ABOVE Two V-shaped ditches augmented the defences of Richborough-*Rutupiae*. This view shows the double ditches protecting the southern defences of the fort. These ditches are wider – the inner one is 10m wide, the outer 5m – than the traditional, shallow obstacle ditches and placed much further out. (Leo Fields)

OPPOSITE PAGE The lighthouse (*pharos*) at Dover-*Dubris* was originally one of a pair on the heights either side of the port. The lower three sections are Roman work of flint-rubble, originally faced in tufa ashlar, with brick bonding courses. The top 6m is medieval, but originally the whole octagonal structure was even higher, reaching some 24.4m. (Esther Carré)

Function

At some stage, probably under Severus Alexander (r. AD 222–35), it had been thought advisable to withdraw troops from the northern frontier and place them in new forts built at Brancaster-*Branoduno*, overlooking the Wash, at Caister-on-Sea close to the mouth of the Yare (*Gariennus*), and at Reculver-*Regulbium* at the approaches to the Thames (*Tamesis*). And so *cohors I Aquitanorum* was stationed at Brancaster-*Branoduno* (RIB 2466), while *cohors I Baetasiorum cR* was assigned to Reculver-*Regulbium* (RIB 2468). The garrison at Caister-on-Sea is unknown. Whether or not these deployments were the result of increasing threat of sea-raiders working northern waters is difficult to say.

In general terms all the Saxon Shore forts occupied locations of a similar nature. They were positioned in sheltered, tidal environments that lay close to, but not directly on, the open sea. Exposed harbours on the open sea have never been thought favourable, and in many cases the sites selected by the Roman surveyors were protected by natural barriers (Brancaster, Reculver, Richborough, Lympne).

Notitia Dignitatum

The *Notitia Dignitatum* is a collection of administrative information, which includes a list of civil and military officials and of military units and their forts in both the eastern and western parts of the empire. Dated to approximately AD 395, the document's internal chronology and purpose are still matters for dispute. Several indirect copies survive, made in the 15th and 16th centuries from a unique Carolingian copy, the *Codex Spirensis*, preserved at Speyer, but long since disappeared.

Chapters arrange the *Notitia Dignitatum*, each one devoted to a high official or army commander, with a schematic picture of his duties and a detailed list of his subordinates and other responsibilities. Thus the *viri illustris magistri officiorum* – Illustrious Master of the Offices – who was responsible for the *scholae* and the arms factories (*fabricae*), is represented by spears, shields, banners, helmets, mail coats and other armour (*ND Occ.* IX_{3-7}). The *vicarius Britanniarum*, on the other hand, is represented by a bird's-eye view of the island with the five provinces of the diocese represented as walled towns (*ND Occ.* XXIII_{3-7}). Within these chapters the document lists officers in both halves of the empire, including commanders of the regional field armies, who are represented by the shield devices of their units listed by seniority and by type, and the frontier commanders by a picture of their sector and a list of garrison units with their station.

Both eastern and western chapters contain a great deal that is earlier than AD 395 (when the empire was divided in this way), but only the western lists have been revised thereafter, which may reflect the supremacy (AD 395–408) and strategy of Stilicho, generalissimo of Honorius. The western chapters include a unique feature, a breakdown by army of all field units. These points suggest that our copy of the *Notitia Dignitatum* might have come from the files of the *magister militum praesentalis*. The lists that survive in the *Notitia Dignitatum* are full of chronological problems: thus the garrison of Hadrian's Wall seems to have survived intact from the early 3rd century AD, whereas the garrisons along the Rhine cannot be earlier than *c.* AD 368.

At the end of the day the most important fact to remember is that such a document would need constant revision. Moreover, although the *Notitia Dignitatum* can be said to generally represent the army of the late 4th century AD,

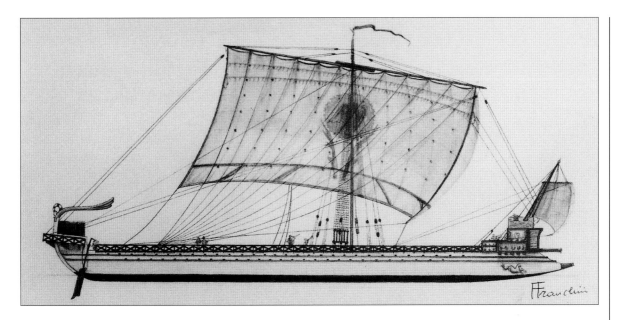

the complete text is composed of elements from different dates, and therefore is not representative of the whole empire at one time. Nonetheless, used with wise caution the document is invaluable, simply because there is nothing to match it for the study of the late Roman army.

For our purposes, the most important senior officer named in the document is *comes litoris Saxonici per Britanniam*. A major problem lies in the fact that the relevant chapter (*ND Occ*. XXVIII) lists only nine sites, when there were at least 11 forts in existence on the Wash–Solent *limes*. Even so, the coastal garrisons listed under the command of the count of the Saxon Shore were stationed at *Othona* (Bradwell), *Dubris* (Dover), *Lemannis* (Lympne), *Branoduno* (Brancaster), *Garianno* (Burgh Castle), *Regulbi* (Reculver), *Rutupis* (Richborough), *Anderidos* (Pevensey), and *Portus Adurni* (Portchester).

In most cases the modern identifications are secure. For example, *Gariannum* seems clearly associated with the river Yare (*Gariennus*) listed by Ptolemaios (*Geographia* 2.3.4). On this basis *Gariannum* has been identified with Burgh Castle, the Shore fort on the banks of a tributary of the Yare. As we know, the forts are striking in their location. All of them were close to the sea and associated with estuaries or coastal waterways, even if now some sites, like Richborough and Pevensey, are far from the sea. The sites are on low ground close to sea level and in all cases were most probably associated with a natural harbour or tidal inlet. In many cases the sites afforded a strategic view of a considerable stretch of coastline.

Anti-pirate defence

In the *Notitia Dignitatum*, as well as the reference to *comes litoris Saxonici*, there are two references to the *litoris Saxonici* on the coast of Gaul. It lists, under the command of the *dux tractus Armoricani et Nervicani* – Duke of the Armorican and Nervian regions – and that of *dux Belgicae secundae*, a parallel chain of garrisons along the north-western coast of Gaul and two of them, one in each command, are described as lying *in litore Saxonico*. They are stationed at *Grannona* and *Marcis* respectively (*ND Occ*. XXXVII$_{14}$, XXXVIII$_6$).

Johnson, who believes that Saxon Shore meant 'shore attacked by Saxons', argues for the wider application of the term along the coast of Gaul. For him, the forts of the Gallic Saxon Shore would have been located on the stretch of coast opposite that defended by their counterparts on the Britannic coast. He suggests, therefore, that all three units commanded by *dux Belgicae secundae* would have

.F L.
INTALL.
COMORD.
PR.

Othona.   Dubrif.

Lemanuif.   Branoduno   Garianno.

Regulbi.   Rutupif.   Anderidof.

Portuadurmi.

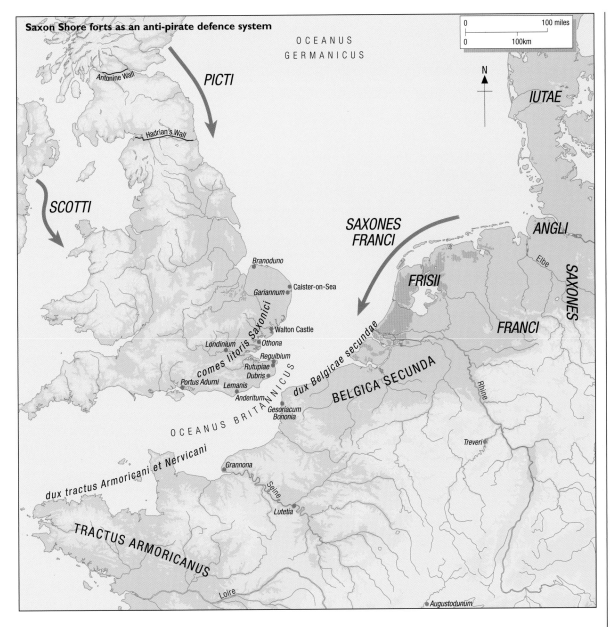

Saxon Shore forts as an anti-pirate defence system

OCEANUS GERMANICUS

PICTI

Antonine Wall

Hadrian's Wall

SCOTTI

IUTAE

ANGLI

SAXONES

SAXONES
FRANCI

FRISII

FRANCI

Elbe

Branoduno

Gariannum Caister-on-Sea

Walton Castle

comes litoris Saxonici

Londinium Othona

Regulbium

Rutupiae

Dubris

Portus Adurni Lemanis

Anderitum

dux Belgicae secundae

BELGICA SECUNDA

Rhine

Gesoriacum
Bononia

OCEANUS BRITANNICUS

Treveri

dux tractus Armoricani et Nervicani

Grannona

Seine

Lutetia

TRACTUS ARMORICANUS

Loire

Augustodunum

been part of the system. To this he adds *Grannona* from the command of the *dux tractus Armoricani et Nervicani* as the westernmost component of the original Saxon Shore system on the Gallic coast. He (1979: 89–90) tentatively proposes that *Grannona* would have been somewhere near the mouth of the Seine, not far from Le Havre. If correct, this would correspond to the positions of Pevensey-*Anderitum* and Portchester-*Portus Adurni*. Thus defined, for Johnson, the Saxon Shore was a single defensive system based on both sides of the Oceanus Britannicus, with the three commanders sharing responsibility for providing effective protection of the north-western coast of Gaul and the south and east coasts of Britannia.

Although the design of the forts is by no means standardized, they have characteristics in common with many of the new linear defences that were being built to protect Gallic urban centres in the late 3rd century AD as a response to barbarian invasions, in particular that of the Franks and Alamanni in AD 276. The consequence of a newly adopted siege mentality in Gaul, these

ABOVE The Shore forts provided safe anchorage for flotillas of the *classis Britannica*, and each had its own garrison of *limitanei*.

OPPOSITE PAGE Insignia of *comes litoris Saxonici per Britanniam*, *Notitia Dignitatum* (Occ. XXVIII$_{3-11}$). Here nine forts are labelled *Othona* (Bradwell), *Dubris* (Dover), *Lemannis* (Lympne), *Branoduno* (Brancaster), *Garianno* (Burgh Castle), *Regulbi* (Reculver), *Rutupis* (Richborough), *Anderidos* (Pevensey), and *Portum Adurni* (Portchester). (Oxford, Bodleian Library, MS Canon Misc. 378, folio 153v)

massive defences are quite different from trends in contemporary military architecture in Britannia. To Johnson this is significant evidence that the Saxon Shore forts are to be seen as part of a unified defensive system to protect Gaul as much as Britannia. Thus this would have seen most of the forts being built between AD 276 and AD 285, perhaps under Probus (r. AD 276–82). The forts already in existence – Brancaster-*Branoduno*, Caister-on-Sea and Reculver-*Regulbium* – would have been incorporated into the system. Such a dating would mean that, whilst he might not have been its designer, Carausius could well have been its first operational commander (Johnson 1979: 68–69, 1983: 211–13).

Johnson views this defensive system of long standing, and is inclined to see the office of *comes maritimi tractus*, mentioned in connection with the events of the *barbarica conspiratio* of AD 367, as a direct precursor of the *comes litoris Saxonici* of the *Notitia Dignitatum*. Thus for Johnson the function of the forts was threefold. They served as fortified naval bases for flotillas, whose task was to intercept sea-raiders; they accommodated units of land forces, which could be deployed rapidly to counter the raiders as they landed; sited as they were on the estuaries of major rivers, they were a deterrent to the penetration inland of raiding parties. To be brief, Johnson's model of the Saxon Shore is one of an integrated, anti-pirate defence system.

Defence against Rome

White, writing earlier than Johnson and before recent reassessments of the dating evidence, saw no archaeological evidence to contradict his view that the forts were built during the reign of Carausius. Yet his hypothesis about the original purpose of the Wash–Solent *limes* still merits discussion.

White reasons that the forts were far more massively built than would have been necessary for the purpose of defending the coasts of south and east Britannia from attacks by Germanic pirates. In his view 'a palisaded camp was all that would have been necessary to deal' with 'a few boatloads of Germans motivated solely by thoughts of plunder' (White 1961: 40). Simultaneously White, unlike Johnson (1979: 6–7), does not discern any evidence, whether documentary or archaeological, that Saxon piracy was a serious threat to

The *ballista* of the late empire was much the same as the 'field artillery' depicted on Trajan's Column (163–164), a two-armed torsion engine that fired bolts. The two metal frames for securing the sinew-springs are enclosed in thin bronze cylinders, thus protecting them from the elements. (Esther Carré)

Britannia in the late 3rd century AD. If that was so and if, as White argues, Carausius built the Saxon Shore forts, they could have had only one credible purpose: to defend Britannia against invasion by the legitimate imperial authorities. In this they were clearly a failure and the defeat of Allectus brought the immediate usefulness of the forts to an end. However, in the second half of the 4th century AD, when there was evidence of a serious Saxon threat, the system could have been reactivated to counter that (White 1961: 19–54).

That the Wash–Solent *limes* was exploited and perhaps expanded by Carausius and Allectus, for instance by the addition of Pevensey-*Anderitum* and Portchester-*Portus Adurni*, to defend Britannia against Maximian and Constantius Chlorus has not received a lot of support in academic circles. But with the publication of new dating evidence from Pevensey, the debate came full circle.

Fulford and Tyers' excavations of the Norman keep in the south-eastern corner of the fort revealed a section of the Roman foundations beneath which were found an array of oak piles. Associated with the foundations were found a coin of Carausius and one of Allectus. Together with the dendrochronological analysis of the piles, which suggested a felling date of AD 280 to AD 300, the coin of Allectus establish what Fulford and Tyers describe as an unequivocal *terminus post quem* of AD 293 for the construction of the fort and a high probability that it was built in the reign of Allectus. The best context, they suggest, for the construction of Pevensey-*Anderitum* and the near contemporary Portchester-*Portus Adurni* and the modernization of other coastal forts in south and east Britannia was the usurpation of Carausius and Allectus.

The dating of Pevensey-*Anderitum* to the reign of Allectus makes it possible that he rather than Carausius was responsible for the development of these defences, given that the loss of Boulogne-sur-Mer (*Gesoriacum Bononia*) in AD 293 would have left Britannia much more vulnerable to invasion by the legitimate regime (Fulford-Tyers 1995). In summary, Fulford and Tyers have revived White's theories, arguing that the usurpers inherited a coastal defence, which already comprised Brancaster-*Branoduno*, Caister-on-Sea, and Reculver-*Regulbium*, and augmented the system by the addition of the other forts during the period AD 293–296.

Fortified ports

Some scholars see no link at all between the Saxon Shore forts and piracy. In particular, Cotterill (1993), developing earlier ideas, proposes an entirely different role for the forts, which places considerable emphasis on their economic function. This alternative, passive view sees the forts, combined with other elements on the north-east and west coasts of Britannia, as part of a chain of fortified ports with no major part to play in maritime or coastal defence.

The location of each Shore fort, near to the mouth of a navigable waterway, did not arise from a need to protect the interior, but instead to facilitate access for both military and commercial shipping. The installations were intended as bases where goods en route for inland garrisons could be offloaded. They could also serve as centres where agricultural and mineral commodities from the region could be collected and shipped onwards for use elsewhere by the army. Many of these goods were destined for the northern frontier, but the forts could also have played a major role in conveying supplies to Gaul and the Rhine frontier.

The supply route for grain from Britannia, re-opened by Iulianus in AD 359 to support his pending campaigns on the lower Rhine, is perhaps one exceptional example of this logistical network in practice. Accounts vary, but something of the order of 600 large vessels were built or commandeered for the task (Ammianus 18.2.3, Julian *Epistulae ad Athenaion* 279–280, Zosimus 3.5.2). The forts may also have served as holding camps for troops in transit. Their importance in this respect would have been greatest at times of military crisis when a secure link between Britannia and Gaul was required. The use of

Naval patrol leaves Dover-*Dubris*

44

Naval patrol leaves Dover-*Dubris*

Vessels of the *classis Britannica* were intended to counter the potential maritime threat to Britannia, but were based mainly in the south and east of the diocese to deter attacks from northern Germania. Active patrols, therefore, swept the Oceanus Britannicus for potential sea-raiders, and early intelligence of a raider's approach allowed the Romans to respond accordingly. The tactic was to trap and destroy the raiding ships when they sailed into the 'narrow sea', or to cut off their retreat by sea if they landed anywhere on the coast.

This scene shows a flotilla of biremes (*liburnae*) leaving Dover-*Dubris*. The distinguishing characteristic of this seagoing vessel is its two banks of oars with one man per oar. It is decked to protect the oarsmen, more from the weather and the swell than the enemy. Approximately 30.5m long by 5.5m wide, it has a complement of 100 oarsmen accompanied by a force of marines. It is also armed with a ram.

In the background is a *pharos*, one of the two lighthouses that overlook the harbour. Built of ashlar-faced rubble with the usual brick bonding courses, at the summit is a fire-beacon housed within a roofed chamber. Pillars of smoke guided shipping by day and flames by night, the light of which was amplified by reflectors of burnished copper. This installation was garrisoned by a detachment sent out from the nearby fort.

Richborough-*Rutupiae* by Theodosius as a place to land his armies in response to the *barbarica conspiratio* of AD 367 illustrates how valuable such defended ports could be (Ammianus 27.8.7).

If the forts were indeed links in a logistical system it would do much to explain the construction of the forts at Brancaster-*Branoduno*, Caister-on-Sea and Reculver-*Regulbium* many decades before the first historical references to piracy in the northern seas. However, despite the silence of the literary sources on the subject of attacks across the northern seas and the lack of specific archaeological evidence, we cannot necessarily assume that Britannia was safe from the Saxons or the Franks. As Bidwell rightly observes, in contrast to the extreme view of Cotterill (1993: 228), 'journeys by raiders would have been feasible if they had rested in deserted coves and inlets along the Gaulish coast, unless we assume that there was immediate Roman supervision and control of every mile of coastline' (1997: 43). As we shall see, their boats were relatively seaworthy and constructed in a way that allowed landing on an open coast. During a sea voyage these were manoeuvred close inshore and navigation was carried out using landmarks. A coastal target, Britannia had always been an accessible landfall for Germanic raiders who dashed across the 'narrow sea' after hugging the Gallic coastline south from northern Germania. The Saxon Shore forts were placed so as to deter such maritime raids.

Reconstruction (Mainz, Museum für Antike Seefahrt) of one of the 4th-century wrecked craft from the middle Rhine. The original (Mainz A) was a wide, flat-bottomed vessel with near vertical sides. It has been identified as a light warship some 21m long and with an oarcrew of 30. (Esther Carré)

Occupation

At few of the sites is there objective evidence for their period of occupation, though coin-finds either from excavation or from chance discoveries are almost exclusively of the late 3rd or 4th century AD. Interior buildings are evident or suggested at several sites, but their plan and layout in all cases is imperfectly known.

Internal buildings

During the Principate, the area within the defences was almost entirely built over, with two main streets (*via praetoria*, *via principalis*) meeting at right angles roughly in the centre of the fort, the location of the headquarters building (*principia*). This traditional layout survived more or less into the middle of the 3rd century AD.

Forts designed from the late 3rd century AD onwards were significantly different from those that had gone before, and this no less so with regards to their internal arrangements. The most striking aspect was the less intensive use of space within the defences. Many buildings tended to be set against the perimeter, where previously this had been the location of the perimeter road (*via sagularis*). From the 4th century AD barrack blocks were constructed against the defences, probably to protect them during a siege. Bathhouses, invariably exterior to earlier forts, were moved within the perimeter, despite the potential fire hazard that they posed. The perimeter buildings often appear to have enclosed a large open courtyard in the centre of the fort, and the *principia* was often absent, at least in a recognizable plan-form, and certainly no longer the focus of garrison life.

The solution to why the layout was so different from that of the Principate probably lies in the many changes to the army itself. During the late Empire much of the administration and logistics became more centralized. Equipment

Internal buildings of the fort at Caister-on-Sea, with building 1 in the foreground and the south wing of a large structure, building 2, beyond. Building 1 was a long strip building, not built before the mid/late 3rd century AD, later to be included in the larger courtyard residence, building 2. (Author's collection)

was often centrally produced and repaired, and food supply was much more tightly controlled. Thus granaries and workshops were no longer needed in such large numbers. Administration was also very much reduced, rendering the *principia* largely unnecessary (Southern-Dixon 2000: 139–41).

This contrast between the internal layout of early and late Roman forts is seemingly apparent in the Saxon Shore forts. As we would expect, Reculver-*Regulbium* offers an almost archetypal plan of an installation of the early 3rd century AD. In the surviving portion the metalled surfaces of the *via principalis*, *via praetoria* and *via sagularis* have been uncovered on a number of occasions during excavation. The stone-built *principia*, complete with underground strong room beneath its *sacellum*, occupied the standard central location, while buildings away from the central range served as barrack blocks, workshops and other ancillary functions (Philp 1996).

Somewhat less is understood of the internal layout of the later group of forts. Some internal structures have been excavated, however, and these appear to be isolated timber-built buildings set amidst vacant areas of ground. For example, at Dover-*Dubris* at least 11 timber-built structures of late Roman date have been found within the defences, of circular, square, oval and sub-rectangular plan (Wilkinson 1994: 76–77). Other scattered elements known within the circuit are metalled roads, a postern with a footbridge, ovens and pits. The 2nd-century bathhouse, built outside the *classis Britannica* fort, was reused within the Shore fort, albeit in a modified form.

Bathhouses are also known within the forts at Richborough-*Rutupiae* and Lympne-*Lemanis*. Traces of mortared floors at the former site also suggest the presence of timber-built structures, probably barrack blocks, and at Portchester-*Portus Adurni*, mortar floors, eaves-drip gullies and the overall layout suggests the presence of at least four small buildings of timber.

Caister-on-Sea, building I looking east towards the south gate, with a corbelled corridor on the south. The purpose of the building is controversial, but the presence of small finds associated with women points to domestic occupation, perhaps an officer's accommodation. (Author's collection)

Garrisons

The late Roman army was divided into several types of troops, a gradation that came to replace the traditional division into legionaries and auxiliaries. At the core of the empire were the household troops (*scholae palatinae*) and other palatine units. Then came the *praesentalis* field army ('in the presence' of the emperor), and after them the regional field armies and the frontier garrisons. The troops of the field armies were known as *comitatenses*, literally the 'accompanying body'. The troops on the frontiers, the ones that concern us here, were called *limitanei* – 'those of the frontier'. By and large they were used to oppose small-scale enemy threats, but could be called upon to assist a *comitatus* operating in the area. Units of *limitanei* transferred to a field army assumed the grade *pseudo-comitatenses*, which does at least indicate that they must still have been considered capable of playing some battlefield role even if only as reserves. This surely makes untenable the highly speculative argument that the *limitanei* were part-time peasant-soldiers, who could not be expected to be much use in time of war. The deterioration in the quality of the *limitanei* was, therefore, a very slow process (Jones 1964: 649–52).

OPPOSITE

Garrison life

Unlike the *comitatenses*, who had no fixed stations, the *limitanei* tended to stay in one place, providing a permanent garrison for various frontier posts. These troops would have been far more integrated in the local community than the *comitatenses* who, in fact, were billeted where convenient. From the early 3rd century AD onwards soldiers were permitted 'to live in wedlock with their wives' (Herodian 3.8.5), and have their families stationed with them. In AD 349, a soldier's family was legally defined as comprising his wife, children and slaves bought from his salary (*CT* 7.1.3).

This scene, set outside the east gate of the fort at Lympne-*Lemanis*, depicts an off-duty member of the garrison, *numerus Turnacensium*, with his family. Although recruited from the Turnacensi tribe, conditions of service for those belonging to this *foederatus* unit were similar to those of regular *limitanei* units. This Germanic warrior, therefore, has his wife and children living within the fort, where rations and shelter are provided for them. The basic peacetime ration, issued from the fort's storehouses (*horrea*), consists of wheaten bread, fresh and cured meat (usually pork), sour wine (*acetum*) and oil. This can be supplemented by a range of foods, such as cheese, pulses, vegetables, fruits, nuts, seafood, fish, poultry and eggs. Unsurprisingly, beer (*cervesa*), made from malted grain, is a popular drink with the Germanic garrison, and our warrior is heading for one of the taverns in the *vicus*.

Yet there seems to be no doubt that the *limitanei* were often held in low esteem. One bishop, at the turn of the 5th century AD, complained bitterly to the emperor about the transfer of a unit of *comitatenses* in his native Cyrenaica to a new role as *limitanei*. It would be a demotion, he wrote, deprived as they would be of their stipends, with no remounts, no military equipment and not enough resources to fight the enemy (Synesius *Epistulae* 78). Often based in forts and watchtowers, the less prestigious *limitanei* carried out duties ranging from internal security, the policing of roads, defence against banditry and raiding, as well as support for provincial officials such as tax collectors and magistrates. Thus Britannia depended on two such garrison bodies. One, the *limitanei* of the north, including Hadrian's Wall, was under the *dux Britanniarum* at York-*Eboracum*. The other, the *limitanei* of the south, including the Saxon Shore forts, was under the *comes litoris Saxonici*.

As a result of their long period of evolution, that is, descendants of the legions and auxiliaries of the Principate, the *limitanei* contained a greater variety of units than the *comitatenses*. These were *legiones* and *cohortes* for the infantry, and *alae* and *equites* for the cavalry. It is difficult to estimate unit sizes, although it does appear that the practice of using detachments (*vexillationes*) led to the reduction in size of the old legions. Richborough-*Rutupiae*, for instance, could not possibly have accommodated more than a fraction of *legio II Augusta* (*ND Occ.* XXVIII$_{19}$), unless the 5,000-strong unit had been much reduced in size or

Room with hypocaust, building 1, Caister-on-Sea. The hypocaust is unusual, being of the channelled type in the centre but with *pilae* set round the edges. It was filled with rammed clay mixed with wheat when it fell into disuse, suggesting it had been used as a grain store. (Author's collection)

Garrison life

was now operating as a series of detachments. It is probable therefore, that *legio Secunda Britannica* (*ND Occ.* V, cf. VII$_{156}$) was one such detachment.

Conversely, the fact that Reculver-*Regulbium* was too large (3.06ha) for a single cohort raises the possibility that it also accommodated naval personnel, as suggested by *(CL)assis (BR)itannica* stamped tiles in addition to *(C)ohors I (B)aetasiorum* tiles. Nevertheless, with a cohort as garrison, its principal function was coastal observation and perhaps interception on land. Fittingly, in the late 2nd century AD, *cohors I Baetasiorum cR* had been stationed at Maryport-*Alauna* on the Cumberland coast (*RIB* 830, 837, 838, 842, 843). It seems probable that the experience it gained patrolling that coast made the unit a promising candidate for similar work attached to the new fort at Reculver-*Regulbium* in the early 3rd century AD. Perhaps we should not forget that ordinary piracy, rather than serious seaborne invasion, could be a real menace. The *Notitia Dignitatum* (*Occ.* XXVIII$_{18}$) records that the unit was still in place at Reculver-*Regulbium* at the end of the 4th century AD.

Both commanders had a number of smaller units known as *numeri*. Raised from barbarian tribes or simply war bands of warriors following their own leaders, these *foederati* had always been hired for campaigns if needed, but the difference in the late 3rd and 4th centuries AD and beyond is that those needs tended to be more permanent. Consequently the *foederati* were liable to be settled across frontier regions, becoming part of the *limitanei*. And so, under the *comes litoris Saxonici*, we find *numerus Fortensium* stationed at Bradwell-*Othona*, *numerus Turnacensium* at Lympne-*Lemanis*, *numerus Abulcorum* at Pevensey-*Anderitum*, and *numerus Exploratorum* at Portchester-*Portus Adurni* (*ND Occ.* XXVIII$_{13, 15, 20, 21}$). Each unit would have been commanded by a Roman *praefectus*.

Extra-mural activity

Small non-military settlements (*vici*) developed close to most Roman forts. The majority were fairly modest in scale and sophistication, and were centres for small-scale industry and trade in goods on a limited basis. Some consisted only of a cluster of strip-buildings beyond the fort gate, but typical elements of more developed *vici* included a bathhouse, temples and a cemetery, alongside a network of domestic-cum-business dwellings and streets. In these members of the garrison could obtain the extras and requirements of social existence not normally available within the fort.

As the result of aerial photography, field walking and geophysical survey, it is apparent that *vici* were associated with many of the Saxon Shore forts. The most extensive extra-mural settlement known thus far is at Brancaster. Here

Classis Britannica

As Britannia was an overseas province, a seaborne arm was necessary for the initial conquest and subsequent defence. Accordingly a provincial fleet, the *classis Britannica*, was formed under a prefect (*praefectus classis Britannicae*), but the Roman Navy was not an independent fighting arm and it operated under the firm control of the army.

The fleet's primary duty was the secure transportation of men and supplies, and the guarding of shipping lanes between Gaul and Britannia (Ammianus 20.1.3, 27.8.6–7). It was thus composed of warships (oared galleys) and merchantmen (sailing vessels). Although it operated out of several harbours in Britannia its principal base (*navalia*) was at Boulogne-sur-Mer (*Gesoriacum Bononia*) in Gaul, where a permanent fort (12.45ha, 30 acres) to house some 4,000 fleet personnel was established in the early 2nd century AD.

Additionally, the *classis Britannica* carried out a number of tasks involved with creating and maintaining the infrastructure of the province. It was employed to build and look after roads and harbours, and three inscriptions (*RIB* 1340, 1944, 1945) attest fleet personnel actually took part in the construction of Hadrian's Wall. Two record their building of a length of the Wall near Birdoswald-*Banna*, while the third records their construction of granaries at Benwell-*Condercum*. There is also evidence to suggest other detachments were engaged in running the ironworks in the Weald of Kent, as well as exploiting its woodland for shipbuilding timber.

LEFT Stele from Niederdollendorf depicting a Frank armed with a *seax*, combing his hair (Bonn, Rheinisches Landesmuseum). Today's Germanic pirates were often yesterday's imperial protectors. One warrior buried on the Danube called himself '*Francus civis, Romanus miles*' (*ILS* 2814): a Frank and a Roman soldier. (Author's collection)

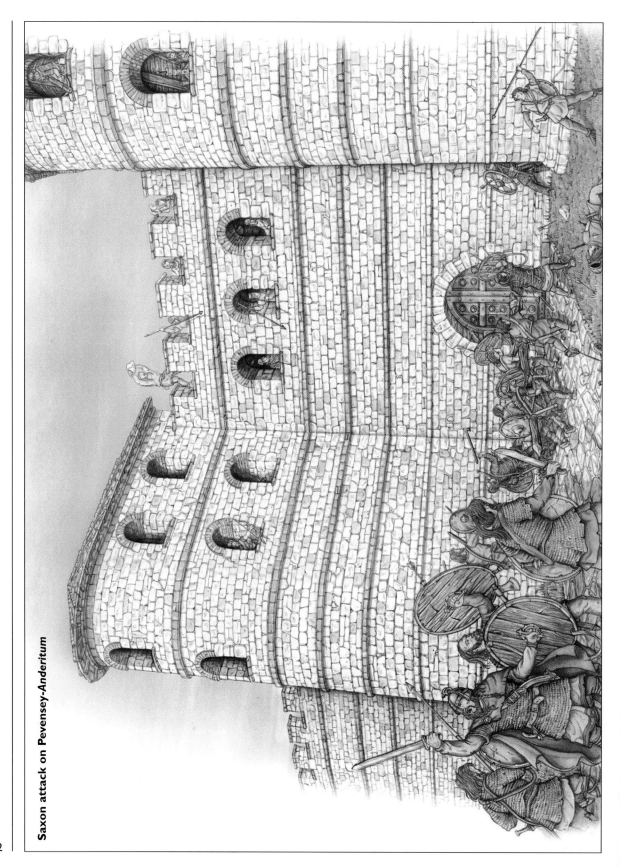

Saxon attack on **Pevensey-Anderitum**

aerial photographs have revealed a complex series of enclosures and associated trackways to the east, west and south of the fort. Subsequent excavation in the western area has led to the interpretation of the enclosures as having been building plots (Hinchliffe-Green 1985).

Similar investigations brought to light significant indications of extra-mural activity around Burgh Castle (Gurney 1995), as is the case for other Shore forts, although here the evidence is based on less intensive surveys. The two exceptions are Pevensey and Portchester, but the negative evidence probably has much to do with the fact that both lay at the end of promontories. On the other hand, there is evidence for civilians and soldiers having lived inside Portchester-*Portus Adurni*, where small-scale industry and butchery took place within its defensive walls (Cunliffe 1975A).

Twilight years

On withdrawing the *comitatenses* from Britannia, Honorius, in his famous rescript of AD 410, advises the *civitates* to organize themselves in a programme of self-help. The Romano-Britons did indeed organize, in an admirable way, in sharp contrast to the response in Gaul, which was subjugated within 50 years by the Franks. Resistance to the Saxons was so stubborn at the turn of the 6th century AD that many migrants returned to their homeland or settled in north-west Gaul. By the middle of the century the Saxon advance began again, this time into south-western Britain with its rich farmlands. This advance was the final phase of the permanent Germanizing of a large part of the British lowlands.

The Romano-Gallic bishop Sidonius Apollinaris, whose grandfather had been an appointee of the Romano-British usurper Constantinus III, attributes several specific characteristics to 5th-century Saxons, about whom he appears to have eyewitness information. He characterizes the Saxons as intrepid and ferocious seafarers. Each, he writes, acted like he was the captain of a pirate ship, launching surprise attacks using 'curving sloops' equipped with oars. He warns his friend Namatius, who is about to set off on a sea voyage, about these brutal adversaries who attack without being spotted and, if seen, giving their pursuers the slip. Pagans, they were reputed to make human sacrifices, killing one in ten of their prisoners by drowning or crucifixion when ready to make sail home (*Epistulae* 8.6.13–15). In another letter (*Epistulae* 8.9.24–27), that to his friend Lampriddius, he describes how they have blue eyes and a distinctive haircut: the front of the head closely shaved with a razor and the hair grown long at the back so as to enlarge the appearance of the face and make the head look smaller. These sound like factual descriptions, not rhetoric or fancy alone, and seem to imply Sidonius had a culturally distinct group in mind.

Hindsight is a luxury: we now appreciate that these Saxon raiders and invaders were not just the three peoples identified by Bede, namely '*Saxones, Angli, et Iutae*' (*HE* 1.15, cf. 5.9, Procopius *Wars* 8.20.7). Frisians and Franks and Wends, a Slavonic people, also represented the incoming Germanic war bands.

Exquisitely carved figurehead (London, British Museum, MME1938.2–2.1) in oak. Dated securely to the 6th century AD, it was dredged from the Scheldt at Appels near Termonde, Belgium, and is believed to have decorated an early Saxon or Frisian warship. (Author's collection)

OPPOSITE PAGE
Saxon attack on Pevensey-*Anderitum*
As the threat from the Saxons grew, those peripheral to that threat probably adopted labour-intensive strategies to provide themselves and their communities with improved security, including the utilization of Roman forts, which still remained largely intact. Such attempts by the Romano-British to stave off a Saxon takeover of lowland Britain, however, were ultimately unsuccessful.

The *Anglo-Saxon Chronicle* relates how a vain defence of the fort at Pevensey-*Anderitum* was made in AD 491, ending in a terrible massacre. The use of the former Saxon Shore fort by the Romano-Britons as a place of refuge ultimately offered no sanctuary. The Saxon chieftains Aelle and Cissa 'besieged *Andredes ceaster* [*Anderitum*] and slew everyone who lived there, so that not one Briton was left' (*ASC* A 491). During the early 5th century AD the inhabitants had, rather inexplicably, built a causeway across the substantial ditch that in Roman times had cut off the west gate from the mainland. This causeway may have done much to render the fort indefensible.

This scene catches the Saxons at the moment of their assault upon the west gate. Having dominated the gate area by missile fire, the attackers are now rushing forward. The storming party is bringing up an improvised ram and some men are armed with crowbars.

Depiction of the *Cornuti* – horned ones – on the Arch of Constantine, Rome, attacking a walled city. These elite soldiers of the *auxilia palatina* were probably recruited from Rhineland Germans. They carry large oval shields and wield spears. The Arch commemorates Constantinus' victory at the Milvian Bridge. (Author's collection)

However the Saxons are best known, along with the Angles and Jutes, as one of 'three most formidable races of Germania' that were later invited (Gildas), in AD 449 under the Jutish warrior-brothers Hengist and Horsa (Bede), to defend Britain by the Romano-British king Vortigern, the *superbus tyrannus* (Gildas *De excidio* 23.1).

Though the exact status of this figure, who is the subject of many legends, remains uncertain, it is widely accepted that Vortigern made use of Hengist and Horsa to protect his kingdom against the Picti and Scotti and rewarded them for their services with a grant of land. They are subsequently said to have turned on their paymaster and invited their compatriots across the northern seas to settle. Vortigern's employment of barbarian mercenaries was by no means original and Germanic *foederati* had cooperated in the defence of military installations even before the Romans withdrew. The *Gallic Chronicle* records that in AD 441 'the provinces of Britain … passed under the control of the Saxons', and archaeological evidence has placed the *adventus Saxonum* – the coming of the Saxons – to around AD 430 (Higham 1993: 168–78).

This domination probably meant only part of Britain. According to Gildas (*De excidio* 20.1) the Romano-Britons still felt it possible to appeal to Aëtius in Gaul in or after AD 446. So it could be claimed that the island was not wholly

Angles, Saxons, and Jutes

Angles, unlike Saxons and Jutes, are named by the 1st-century Roman historian Tacitus (*Germania* 40.1), and formed in his time part of a confederation of Germanic peoples known as the Suevi. Yet Saxons are mentioned in later Roman sources as raiders on the empire. They came from lands around the lower Elbe and were closely linked with the Angles, who lived immediately to the north of them. By linguistic implication, the Jutes were taken to come from Jutland, though archaeological evidence from Jutish Kent indicates, compared with other parts of Britain, the prevalence of a far more elaborate culture closely related to that of the Franks. Incidentally, the collective term 'Anglo-Saxon', by which these tribes are commonly known, is that coined by the Normans as a legal definition of the people they had conquered.

It is often very difficult to distinguish between the graves of late-Roman soldiers of Germanic descent and those of continental Saxons, as weapons, belt buckles and shields are often identical. There was a Saxon saying that warfare was proper for a nobleman, and male burials in Britain during the pagan period were often accompanied by war gear. Chieftains and more important noblemen would possess a sword, shield and spear(s), a mail-shirt and helm. The early Saxon mail-shirt (*byrnie*) reached to just below the waist and had short sleeves, and the helmet was commonly of the *spangenhelm* type, where the bowl was made of several parts, held together by reinforcing clasps that covered the joins. Noblemen of middling rank may have possessed a helmet, perhaps a sword, and a shield and spear(s). Similar to the Roman *spatha*, the sword was a long, straight, two-edged weapon designed primarily for cutting. It was an expensive item requiring skill in its production and as a result highly prized. As Evans says, 'the sword should be seen as the weapon that can be associated with the wealthier or more successful members of a war band' (2000: 39).

The most common weapon, however, was the spear. The lowest-ranking warriors would have been equipped with just a shield and spear(s), and perhaps a secondary weapon such as an axe or, more usually, a *seax*, the long single-edged knife from which the Saxons apparently derive their name. Primarily an everyday tool, in battle it could be used to finish off a felled opponent. Although the main weapon was the spear, not only for the peasant but also for the professional warrior and even the nobility, all warriors carried the *seax*, as the wearing of a knife may have been a symbol of a weapon-owning freeman. The *seax* appears to have been worn across the stomach, blade uppermost, with the hilt at the right, to make it easy to draw (Pollington 1996: 149). Saxon shields, round or near-round ovals in shape, were stoutly made of solid planks of linden, alder or willow wood. The central hole through which the handgrip was fixed was protected by a heavy projecting iron boss, which could be used as an offensive weapon. As the author of the 6th-century *Strategikon* says, 'they prefer fighting on foot and rapid charges' (11.3.2). While bows were widely used by the continental Saxons, the insular Saxons seem to have used the bow mainly for hunting, displaying certain disdain for its use in battle. Bows were mainly made of yew, elm or ash.

politically independent of the empire even then. It is more likely that there was still a group of people in Britain as late as the mid-5th century AD that held hopes of Roman intervention, but these hopes were unrealized. Gildas says the new arrivals came 'in three, as they say in their language, *cyulis* (keels), warships (*longis navibus*) in our language' (*De excidio* 22.3). Likewise the later *Anglo-Saxon Chronicle* (A 449, 477, 495, 501), written with notable economy of detail to support the political aspirations of the late Saxon kings of Wessex, suggests that they came in groups of two to five *cyulis*.

Clearly the size of these 'keels' is of importance here, and good evidence comes in the shape of a late 4th-century boat deposited at Nydam Mose, Jutland. Deliberately sunk, the boat was laden with war booty, including over 100 swords. The boat itself was some 23.7m long, 3.5m broad and 1.2m deep. Warrior-oarsmen, 30 in number, propelled this open vessel, while a steersman controlled it by means of a large steering-paddle on the starboard ('steer-board') side. The keel-less hull was built from 11 broad oaken planks, and was furnished with barb-shaped rowlocks, 15 per side, lashed to the gunwales. The overlapping strakes were fastened with iron clinch-nails. The hull was rendered watertight by jamming pieces of tarred wool into the overlaps between the clinker-laid planks. There was no deck but the transverse timbers are shaped in a way that makes them suitable for supporting loose floorboards (Rieck 2000: 60). Procopius tells us that Angle warships of his day 'do not use sail for seafaring, they only use oars' (*Wars* 8.20.31) and, to all intents and purposes, the Nydam ship was a sleek, seagoing rowing boat.

The early settlements in eastern Britain would seem to have been on a very small scale. The evidence of cemeteries shows gradual cultural integration, represented by women's dress brooches (crossbow- and trumpet-shaped) similar to those found in north-west Germania, which might reflect intermarriage. At the same time men were buried with their weapons and 5th-century versions of late-Roman military belts. Ethnically these warriors were Saxons and Franks and

Intercepting Saxon pirates

Intercepting Saxon pirates

The Saxons were equipped with ideologies that positively encouraged military adventurism, and a surplus of well-equipped warriors, some of whom had a tradition of service in Roman armies or of raiding Roman territory. As the extensive coastline of Britannia was very exposed to sea-raiders, its protection required the services of special naval surveillance craft swift and manoeuvrable enough to chase and intercept the equally swift Saxon vessels. In these foggy waters the element of surprise was important, and these scouting-skiffs (*scaphae exploratoriae*) had their hulls, sails, rigging and even the crews' uniforms camouflaged in blue-green (Vegetius *Epit.* 4.37).

Nicknamed *picati* – painted – each vessel, a substantial craft some 25m in length, is powered by 40 oarsmen arranged in one rank, 20 oars a side. Each is carvel-built, whereby flushed planks were laid edge to edge and locked together by using close-set mortise-and-tenon joints. The internal strengthening frames were added afterwards. Pine, larch and fir were recommended for shipbuilding (Vegetius *Epit.* 4.34), although oak appears to have been favoured for ships plying rough, northern waters. It is possible that this type of light warship was similar to one of the 4th-century wrecks discovered on the middle Rhine at Mainz.

Designed to be effective in coastal shallows and deep water alike, the Saxon warships are open-hulled rowing vessels measuring some 23.5m in length. Each is propelled by 30 oars and steered by a large paddle-shaped side-rudder placed near the stern. Belonging to the Nordic boat-building tradition, they are clinker-built rather than carvel-built. The overlapping oaken planks are riveted together with iron clinch-nails and caulked with pieces of tarred wool to render the hull watertight. Their spines consist of an extra-heavy bottom plank to which are fixed high, curving stem- and stern-posts, which, coupled with their wide hulls with good distance from the gunwale to the waterline, enable them to withstand heavier seas and violent storms. Having no keels means they can be beached with ease.

Whereas the older hull-first construction used by the Romans was hugely expensive in both timber, time and skill, especially if oak was employed, the subsequent frame-first hull used by the Saxons required much less timber, was quicker, and demanded fewer highly skilled shipbuilders.

may well have been recruited by the Romano-British *civitates* from the disintegrating field armies, or units of *foederati* from northern Gaul and the Rhineland, the only pool of equipped and trained men available to them. These warrior communities were dispersed in much the same area as the garrisons of the Wash–Solent *limes* and they may have been intended to perform a similar function, protecting the south and east coasts from sea-raiders. The archaeological evidence also shows that the forts at Richborough-*Rutupiae* and Portchester-*Portus Adurni* were partially occupied by Germanic barbarians whose exact status is unknown (Cunliffe 1968: 250, 1975B: 301).

The evidence is consistent with the view that these warrior inhumations reflect a late diocesan and early post-diocesan deployment of small numbers of soldiers equipped and recruited in Gaul and the Rhineland. In the course of the 5th and 6th centuries AD, however, Germanic material culture and urned cremation became prevalent across southern and eastern Britain, but the scale of this immigration is difficult to assess since it is possible that Romano-Britons had become acculturated to Germanic ways (Higham 1993: 113–19, 174–76).

Bronze model of a Roman galley-prow (London, British Museum, PRB1856.7-1.29) from London. The vessel's stem-post is decorated with a curving goose-head, while its keel terminates as a wolf-headed ram. Its bears the inscription, in retrograde, 'Ammilla Augusta the Fortunate' (*AMMILLA AUG FELIX*), the warship's name. (Esther Carré)

The sites today

The physical settings of the Saxon Shore forts have been much changed since Roman times. Visitors to the sites at Richborough, Lympne and Pevensey, for instance, will find these sites firmly landlocked. By contrast, Walton Castle has fallen victim to the sea, while Reculver has been partially destroyed by the same process of coastal erosion. Only Portchester retains a landscape setting similar to that in the 3rd century AD. Not surprisingly the underlying factors influencing coastal morphology have been changing sea-levels, which in south-eastern Britain during the 1st century AD were approximately 3 to 4m below those at present, the destruction of the coast – erosion – and the mechanism of accretion – the siltation or drainage of land – which result in the retreat of the sea.

Brancaster

The site of the fort, lying between the north Norfolk villages of Brancaster and Brancaster Staithe, is known only from crop marks. It is now located on a raised platform, roughly 500m from the North Sea, on the edge of a broad swathe of tidal marsh.

Caister-on-Sea

The remains of the fort are tucked away in the midst of a modern housing estate, were a short section of the south wall and south gate are exposed to view. In Roman times the fort lay close to the south-east tip of an island roughly 10km square in what was then the so-called Great Estuary.

Robbed facing stones from the fort at Brancaster-*Branoduno* are seen here reused in the south wall of the 12th-century chancel of St Mary the Virgin, Brancaster. The ashlar blocks were probably taken from the fort's defences. (Author's collection)

Burgh Castle

Situated on a raised tongue of land on the edge of the Norfolk Broads, the fort overlooks the much-diminished 'Great Estuary', upon whose shores it once stood. Three sides of the defences now remain, including the entire east wall.

Walton Castle

Once standing on a cliff a little to the north of Felixstowe, Suffolk, the fort entirely succumbed to coastal erosion in the 18th century and is now known only from antiquarian drawings and descriptions. However, during exceptionally low tides rocks, some of which are the remnants of the Roman defences, are visible at a distance from the beach beneath the cliff line at Walton.

Bradwell

Situated on the edge of the Dengie Marshes, Essex, little has survived of the Roman fort at Bradwell. It is now best known for the East Saxon chapel of St Peter, at the place named *Ythancaester* by Bede (*HE* 3.22), which was built around AD 652 of material robbed from the defences of the fort. The chapel presently overlooks the tidal mudflats of the Blackwater estuary, but in Roman times substantial tidal inlets to the north and south defined the promontory on which the fort stood.

Reculver

The site is well known to mariners plying the Thames estuary as 'Twin Towers Reculver', being recorded as such on Admiralty Charts, leading from the Four Fathoms Channel into Margate Road. The twin towers belong to the medieval church of St Mary, now disused and abandoned, standing within the site of the

LEFT The church of St Peter and St Paul, Burgh Castle. The round bell tower, an architectural feature peculiar to some Norfolk churches, contains flint, brick and tile robbed from the nearby Saxon Shore fort. (Author's collection)

RIGHT North wall, chapel of St Peter at Bradwell-*Othona*. This view shows the Saxon re-use of Roman brick and stone. This was one of Cedd's missionary churches incorporated into the fort built in the days of Roman power to keep the forefathers of the English out of Britain. (Esther Carré)

Roman fort, half of which has been washed away by coastal erosion. The single most impressive architectural feature of the fort still open to view is the south gate.

Richborough

The site has a complex history of Roman occupation, all of which is reflected in its visible remains. As well as the substantial remains of the Shore fort, an amphitheatre survives as a slight hollow 400m to the south-west, and a cemetery and two small Romano-Celtic temples are known. Within the perimeter of the stone-built fort lie the remains of the so-called Great Monument and the prominent triple ditches, which once surrounded the 3rd-century watchtower that replaced it. The circuit of the fort itself survives on three sides, the east wall having collapsed into the river Stour.

Dover

Only small sections of the enceinte have been excavated, all of which are fragments of the south-western portion of the Shore fort overlying the demolished north-east corner of the earlier *classis Britannica* installation. The best-exposed section is that showing part of the south wall, complete with interval tower, cutting across the east gate of the earlier fort.

Lympne

The remnants of the fort are situated on the slopes of an ancient degraded cliff overlooking Romney Marsh, Kent. During the Roman period the site overlooked a major tidal inlet that opened to the sea near West Hythe. The defences only survive in fragmentary form, in many cases displaced by landslips from their original locations.

Medieval church of St Mary at Reculver-*Regulbium*, first founded around AD 670. This was built close to the then ruined fort and later extended, in particular with the addition of the massive twin towers in *c.*1200. Note the proximity of the shoreline. (Leo Fields)

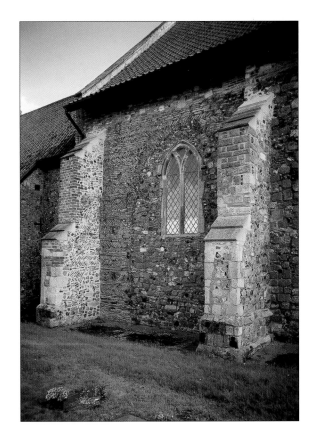

Pevensey

The largest of the Saxon Shore forts, that at Pevensey, East Sussex, remains to this day an impressive monument. The south-east corner of the Roman circuit is now occupied by the medieval castle, first established by the Normans, while approximately two-thirds of the original circuit of 760m has survived to the present day. The fort now stands land-locked on a slightly elevated tongue of land approximately 1km from the sea. At the time of its construction, however, it was positioned at the end of a raised peninsula and surrounded by a shallow coastal marsh.

Portchester

Portchester, at the head of Portsmouth Harbour, Hampshire, has the longest and most continuous post-Roman history of occupation of any of the Saxon Shore forts. There was extensive use of the site during Saxon, medieval and modern periods, and it only ceased to function as a military installation during the early 19th century when its last roles included barracks, stores base and prisoner-of-war camp. This fact is reflected in the existing monument's fabric, which exhibits numerous repairs, alterations and additions spanning the centuries. Particularly prominent within the Roman circuit are the Norman keep and medieval gatehouse inserted in the north-west corner, and the church in the south-east quarter.

Useful contact information

English Heritage
Tel.   +44 (0)870 333 1181
Fax   +44 (0)179 341 4926
Email customers@english-heritage.org.uk
Web   www.eng-h.gov.uk

LEFT The church of St John the Baptist, Reedham, incorporates large quantities of Roman brick and tile in its fabric, indicating that a substantial Roman structure stood nearby. The locality would have lain on the shores of the 'Great Estuary', and has been suggested to be a lighthouse or watchtower. (Author's collection)

RIGHT Aerial view of Portchester-*Portus Adurni*. The topography has changed little here, and on the east side the sea still laps up to the walls. The Roman curtains and towers are almost intact, with the addition of a Norman keep and medieval gatehouse in the north-west corner. (Author's collection)

Glossary

Augustus	Imperial title designating the two senior members of Tetrarchy
Ballista/ballistae	Light, twin-armed torsion engine firing bolts
Bonding courses	Horizontal courses of stone, brick or re-used tile built at vertical intervals up wall in order to tie the shallow facing into the mass of the core
Caesar	Imperial title designating the two junior members of Tetrarchy
Carvel-built	Constructed with hull planks flush or edge to edge
Civitas/civitates	Community of fellow citizens (*cives*)
Clinker-built	Constructed with planks or strakes overlapping
Comes/comites	'Companion' – translated as count, commander of a field force
Comes domesticorum	Commander of *domestici* protecting the emperor
Currach	Seagoing vessel made of hide
Diocese	Super-province
Dux/duces	'Leader' – translated as duke, commander of designated sector of frontier
Foederati	Paid barbarians, under their ethnic leaders, serving Roman emperor
Iaculus/iacula	*Ballista* bolt
Knot	Speed of one nautical mile an hour
Laeti	Barbarians settled on Roman territory and obliged to serve in army
Magister equitum	Master of Cavalry – title given to senior Roman commander
Magister militum	Master of Soldiers – collective title for both services
Magister peditum	Master of Infantry – title given to senior Roman commander
Numerus/numeri	'Number, mass' – unit of *foederati*
Nautical mile	Distance equivalent to the length of one degree of latitude
Petit appareil	Type of wall construction using stone cut into small, neat cubes
Tegula/tegulae	Flat roof-tile with flanged edges along the long sides

Bibliography

Bartholomew, P., 1984, 'Fourth-century Saxons' *Britannia* 15: 169–85

Bidwell, P., 1997, *Roman Forts in Britain* London: Batsford/English Heritage

Breeze, D. J., 1984, 'Demand and supply on the northern frontier', in R. Miket and C. Burgess (eds.), *Between and Beyond the Walls: Essays in Honour of George Jobey* Edinburgh: Edinburgh University Press: 265–76

Cotterill, J., 1993, 'Saxon raiding and the role of the late Roman coastal forts of Britain' *Britannia* 24: 227–39

Cunliffe, B. (ed.), 1968, *Fifth Report on the Excavations at the Roman Fort at Richborough, Kent* London: Research Report of the Society of Antiquaries of London 23

Cunliffe, B., 1975A, *Excavations at Portchester Castle I: Roman* London: Research Report of the Society of Antiquaries of London 32

Cunliffe, B., 1975B, *Excavations at Portchester Castle 2: Saxon* London: Research Report of the Society of Antiquaries of London 33

Dark, K. R., 2000, *Britain and the End of the Roman Empire* Stroud: Tempus

Evans, S. S., 1997, 2000, *Lords of Battle: Image and Reality of the* comitatus *in Dark-Age Britain* Woodbridge: Boydell Press

Fields, N., 2003, *Fortress 002: Hadrian's Wall* AD *122–410* Oxford: Osprey

Fulford, M. and Tyers, I., 1995, 'The date of Pevensey and the defence of an *Imperium Britanniarum*' *Antiquity* 69: 1009–14

Grainge, G., 2005, *The Roman Invasions of Britain* Stroud: Tempus

Gurney, D., 1995, *Burgh Castle: the Extra-mural Survey* Dereham: Norfolk Archaeologial Unit

Haywood, J., 1991, *Dark Age Naval Power: a Re-assessment of Frankish and Anglo-Saxon Seafaring Activity* London: Routledge

Higham, N. J., 1992, 1993, *Rome, Britain and the Anglo-Saxons* London: Seaby

Hinchliffe, J., and Green, C. S., 1985, *Excavations at Brancaster, 1974 and 1977* Norwich: Norfolk Museums and Archaeology Service (East Anglian Archaeology Report 23)

Johnson, S., 1979, *The Roman Forts of the Saxon Shore*[2] London: Elek

Johnson, S., 1983, *Late Roman Fortifications* London: Batsford

Jones, A. H. M., 1964, *The Later Roman Empire: a Social, Administrative and Economic Survey* 2 vols. Oxford: Oxford University Press

Laing, J., 2000, *Warriors of the Dark Age* Stroud: Sutton

McGrail, S., 1995, 'Romano-Celtic boats and ships: characteristic features' *International Journal of Nautical Archaeology* 24: 139–45

Mason, D. J. P., 2003, *Roman Britain and the Roman Navy* Stroud: Tempus

Maxfield, V. A. (ed.), 1989, *The Saxon Shore* Exeter: University of Exeter Press

Nicasie, M. J., 1998, *Twilight of Empire: the Roman Army from the Reign of Diocletian to the Battle of Adrianople* Amsterdam: Gieben.

Nischer, E. C., 1923, 'The army reforms of Diocletian and Constantine and their modifications up to the time of the *Notitia Dignitatum*' *Journal of Roman Studies* 13: 1–55

Parker, H. M. D., 1933, 'The legions of Diocletian and Constantine' *Journal of Roman Studies* 23: 175–89

Pearson, A., 2002, *The Roman Shore Forts: Coastal Defences of Southern Britain* Stroud: Sutton

Philp, B. J., 1996, *The Roman Fort at Reculver* Dover: Kent Archaeological Rescue Unit

Pollington, S., 1996, *The English Warrior from Earliest Times to 1066* Hockwold: Anglo-Saxon Books

Rieck, F., 2000, 'Seafaring in the North Sea region, AD 250–850', in Pentz, P. *et al.* (eds.) *Kings of the North Sea, AD 250–850* Newcastle: Tyne and Wear Museums, 55-66

Severin, T., 1978, *The Brendan Voyage* London: Hutchinson

Southern, P., and Dixon, K. R., 1996, 2000, *The Late Roman Army* London: Routledge

White, D. A., 1961, Litus Saxonicum: *the British Saxon Shore in Scholarship and History* Madison, WI: University of Wisconsin Press

Whittaker, C. R., 1994, 1997, *Frontiers of the Roman Empire: a Social and Economic Study* Baltimore: John Hopkins University Press

Wilkinson, D. R. P., 1994, 'Excavations on the White Cliffs Experience site, Dover 1988–91'. *Archaeologia Cantiana* 114: 51–148

Index

Figures in **bold** refer to illustrations

Allectus 11, 43
Ammianus 11, 27
Angles 55
Anglo-Saxon Chronicle 53, 55
Arcadius, Emperor 13, **13**, 14
Arch of Constantine **54**
Arch of Galerius **12**
artillery 27, **42**
Aurelius Victor 10

ballistae 27, **42**
barbarica conspiratio (AD 367) 11–13, 45
Bede 53, 54
Bidwell, P. 45
Bradwell-*Othona* 24, 29–32, **59**
Brancaster: church of St Mary the Virgin **58**
Brancaster-*Branoduno*
   architectural style and date 24
   construction 19, 21
   defences 25, **25**
   facing stones robbed from **58**
   garrison 38
   vicus at 51–53
Brendan, St 15
Britannia
   administration and government
     9-10, 48, 53
   history 10–17
   Saxon incursions 53–54
   Saxon settlements 55–57
Burgh Castle-*Gariannum*
   architectural style and date 24
   church of St Peter and St Paul **59**
   construction 19, **20**
   defences 28–29, **28–29**, **33**
   fort **28**
   situation **27**
   vicus 53

Caister-on-Sea
   architectural style and date 24
   defences **18**, 24, 25–27
   garrison 38
   internal buildings **46–48**
   situation **27**
Carausius, Mausaeus 10–11, 42, 43
classis Britannica 44, 51
Claudian 13, 14, 16
comites (sing. *comes*): definition 12
Constantinus I, Emperor 9, 12
Constantinus III, Emperor 16–17
Constantius I Chlorus, Emperor 10, **10**,
   11, 43
construction methods 19, **21–23**

Cotterill, J. 43
curtain walls **7**, **22**, **29**, **61**

Diocletianus, Emperor 9
ditches **24–25**, **35**, 37
Dover-*Dubris* 24, 34, **36**, **44**, 47
duces (sing. *dux*): definition 11–12

Eutropius 10

Faenza Mosaic **14**
food and drink 48
Franks 51
Fulford, M. 43
Fullofaudes 11

garrisons and garrison life 38, 47–50, **49**
gateways **26**, 27, **35**
Gaul 17, 39–42, **41**, 53
Gildas 11, 13, 14, 15, 16, 17, 54–55
Gildo 14, 15
Grannona 39, 41, **41**
Great Estuary **27**

Hengist 54
Holland, Philemon 32
Honorius, Emperor 13, **13–14**, 16, 17, 53
Horsa 54
human resources 21–23
hypocausts **48**

internal buildings 46–47, **46–48**

Johnson, S. 39–42
Jutes 55

lighthouses **36**, **44**
London-*Londinium* **10**
Lympne-*Lemanis* **49**
   architectural style and date 24
   construction 19, 20, 21
   defences 34–35
   internal buildings 47

Marcis 39
Maximian, Emperor 10–11, 43

Nectaridus 12–13
Notitia Dignitatum 38–39, **40**

Obelisk of Karnak **13**

Pevensey-*Anderitum*
   construction 19, **22**
   date 24, 43
   defences 35
   gateways 26, **27**
   Saxon attack on **52**
Portchester-*Portus Adurni*
   aerial view **61**
   date 24, 43
   defences **7**, 19, 37
   garrison 57

   life within 53
   Watergate **26**, 27
Procopius 17, 55

rampart-walks **33**
raw materials 19–21
Reculver-*Regulbium*
   architectural style and date 24
   church of St Mary **60**
   construction 20–21, **22**
   defences 32–33
   garrison 38
   internal layout 47
Reedham: church of St John **61**
Richborough-*Rutupiae*
   architectural finds from **5**
   and *barbarica conspiratio* (AD 367) 45
   construction 19, 21, **21**, **23**
   date 24
   defences and plan **30–32**, 33, **34–35**, 37
   garrison 48–50, 57
   internal buildings 47
   Great Monument 4, 21
Roman Army **12**, **50**
   administration and logistics 38–39,
     43–45, 46–47
   limitanei 47–50, **49**
   types of troops 47

Saxon Shore
   definition 4
   location of forts **6**, **41**
Saxons 11, **52**, 53–5
   raids 39–42, **44**, 45, **56**
   weapons and equipment **51**, 55
Severin, Tim 15
ships and boats
   currachs 15, **15**
   decorations **5**, **57**
   liburnae 39, **44–45**, 45, **50**
   merchantmen **30–31**
   Saxon 55, **56**
   scouting-skiffs **56**
Sidonius Apollinaris 53
Stilicho, Flavius 4, 13–16, **14**, **16**, 17

Tarrutienus Paternus 21
Theodosius I, Emperor 12, 13, **13**, 45
Theodosius, Flavius 12–13
towers **7**, **26**, 27, **33–34**, **61**
Trajan's Column **42**
Tyers, I. 43

Valentinianus I, Emperor 11
Vegetius 4
vici 50–53
Vitruvius 19
Vortigern 54

Walton Castle **29**
White, D.A. 42–43

Zosimus 13, 17